W9-BIE-195

Unlocking the Scriptures for You

HEBREWS

Stephen M. Hooks

**STANDARD
BIBLE STUDIES**

STANDARD PUBLISHING
Cincinnati, Ohio   11-40114

Unless otherwise noted, all Scripture quotations are from the *Holy Bible: New International Version,* ©1973, 1978, 1984 by the International Bible Society. Used by permission of Zondervan Bible Publishers and the International Bible Society.

Library of Congress Cataloging in Publication Data:

Hooks, Stephen M.
   Hebrews / Stephen M. Hooks.
      p. cm. — (Standard Bible studies)
   ISBN 0-87403-174-5
   1. Bible. N.T. Hebrews—Commentaries. I. Title. II. Series.
BS2775.3.H66 1990
227'.8707—dc20   90-31546
                                                              CIP

CONTENTS

Author's Preface

This commentary is applicational with a capital *A*. Its design is to capture the essence of the text and to communicate it to the popular Christian audience. Those looking for detailed, verse-by-verse comment will be disappointed. There is no attempt to exhaust the text, only to understand it. The reader will find more exposition than exegesis, more homiletics than hermeneutics. Rather than debate the text, we will seek to distill it into its essential message and let it speak compellingly to the modern believer.

We are simply trying to do for our generation what the author of Hebrews was trying to do for his: to demonstrate the relevance of Christ for contemporary humanity. *Today* is a favorite word for our author. He is continually quoting from ancient Biblical texts and suggesting their implication for his own age. His method is to explain God's Word in the past with a view toward its meaning for the present. This, too, is our quest. To be sure, this brief study is not the last word on Hebrews. Our hope is that it will prove to be a timely word.

Introduction

A first reading of the book of Hebrews can be a frustrating experience for the modern Christian. With its long, drawn-out arguments and frequent references to priests, sacrifices, and angels, the book seems almost otherworldly in language and style. Some readers might identify with the young Charles Haddon Spurgeon, who recalled sitting through a series of sermons on the book and confessed, "I wished frequently that the Hebrews had kept their Epistle to themselves, for it sadly bored a poor Gentile lad."

Those who stay with the book, however, do not go unrewarded. There is truth here that is vital and relevant. Released from its archaic trappings, the message of this book strikes a responsive chord in the hearts of all believers. It is a Christ-book from cover to cover. In the opening verses, Jesus is presented as the consummate Word of God, and, in the closing verses, He is praised as the Christ "to whom be glory for ever and ever."

Recipients of the Letter

They Are Jewish

"To the Hebrews" is the address posted on this letter. Though this title may not have been original to the book, it does have the support of the earliest known manuscripts and is consistent with the predominantly Jewish tone of the epistle's contents. The author presupposes of his readers an unquestioning acceptance of the Old Testament as the authoritative Word of God, quoting frequently and arguing consistently from the Jewish Scriptures as reason for and example of the case he wishes to make. He also presupposes of his readers an intricate knowledge of Jewish religious ritual. Indeed, his entire affirmation of the superiority of Christianity is made in contrast with, and as an alternative to, Judaism. It would be difficult to explain the extent to which the author compares Christianity to Judaism for an audience that was not faced with just such a choice.

They Are Christians

Even more important than the ethnic status of the book's recipients is their spiritual status. These Jews are also Christians—believers, converts to the way of Christ.

1. *They have accepted the faith.* The author frequently addresses the readers as "brothers" (Hebrews 3:1; 10:19; 13:22) and regularly employs the common plurals "we," "us," and "our" when referring to the Christian experience (Hebrews 3:1; 4:1, 2, 3; 8:1; 10:19-25). They "have been evangelized" (Hebrews 4:2—author's translation), have "come to share in Christ" (Hebrews 3:14), are "in the body" (Hebrews 13:3—NASB, KJV), and "have a great high priest who has gone through the heavens, Jesus the Son of God" (Hebrews 4:14).

2. *They are suffering because of the faith.* These Jewish converts have been paying a price for their allegiance to Jesus Christ. Their discipleship has come at the cost of public ridicule, confiscation of personal property, and, for some, even imprisonment (Hebrews 10:32-34). It does not appear, however, that they have suffered to the point of martyrdom (Hebrews 12:4).

3. *They are in danger of forsaking the faith.* It is this very danger that seems to provide the occasion for the writing of the book. The author repeatedly encourages the Hebrew Christians to hold firmly to the faith (Hebrews 4:14-16), to exercise diligence and patience until the end (Hebrews 6:11, 12), and not to grow weary and lose heart (Hebrews 12:3). Balancing these encouragements are stern warnings against drifting away (Hebrews 2:1), failing to enter their "rest" through disobedience (Hebrews 4:1-11), throwing away their confidence (Hebrews 10:35), spurning Christ and insulting the Spirit of grace (Hebrews 6:4-8; 10:26-31), and falling away from the living God (Hebrews 3:12). In the face of this grave danger, the author calls upon his readers to look to Jesus as the consummate model of faithful endurance (Hebrews 3:1-6; 12:1-3).

The Author of the Letter

"Only God knows" was Origen's famous answer to the question, "Who wrote Hebrews?" That third-century answer is just as valid today. The ancient church of the East held to Pauline authorship, as did Clement of Alexandria (late second century). In the West, Tertullian held that it was Paul's associate Barnabas who was the author, and it was not until the fourth century that Pauline authorship was generally accepted. Apollos, Luke, Clement of Rome, Priscilla, Philip, Peter, Silvanus (Silas), Ariston, and Jude are among the many other candidates who have been suggested as the possible author of the book.

Though the name of the author eludes us, other things about him emerge from the pages of his book. He was probably a second-generation Christian (Hebrews 2:3, 4) and was very knowledgeable of the Greek language (the Greek of Hebrews is some of the finest in the New Testament). His rich vocabulary suggests that he was a learned man, and his style of writing suggests that he was skilled in rhetoric. He was well-versed in the Old Testament Scriptures and was familiar with first-century Jewish exegesis. He was also well-acquainted with his readers (Hebrews 13:22-25) and had a deep concern for their spirituality (Hebrews 6:1-12).

In spite of his anonymity, the author of Hebrews leaves behind him a significant spiritual legacy. Among the many contributions of his book to the Christian faith, his portrait of Christ as the great high priest and perfect sacrifice for sin is unique in the New Testament.

Purpose of the Letter

Determining the purpose of a Biblical book can be a precarious task. Generally speaking, though, the content and form of Scripture hold the keys to unlocking its intent with the author's own statements serving as the court of final appeals. Fortunately for the book of Hebrews, all of these elements come together to suggest a common answer. The writer states his purpose in Hebrews 13:22 when he says, "Brothers, I urge you to bear with my word of exhortation, for I have written you only a short letter." If *word of exhortation* means here, as in Acts 13:15, a homily, it would suggest that this letter is also a sermon—exhortations from Scripture for the purpose of arousing faith and changing conduct. The letter itself possesses all the elements of a sermon. There is the systematic use of Scripture in support of a theme or proof of a point, coupled with frequent appeals, encouragements, reproofs, and warnings.

The essential nature of the book of Hebrews may thus be summarized in the following fashion:

1. *Content:* The superiority and sufficiency of Jesus Christ as Word of God and Way to God.
2. *Form:* A sermon—a formal summons to conviction and conduct on the basis of Scripture.
3. *Intent:* That the readers might not forsake Christ but continue to abide in Him unto their salvation.

By discovering the book's purpose, we also establish its relevance for the modern Christian. Twentieth-century Christians, like first-century Christians, are besieged by constant pressures to forsake Christ for other religions, philosophies, and life-styles. There is no shortage of alternatives to faith in Christ as the key to the fulfillment and arrival of humankind. The issue raised by this book remains the essential issue of life: "Who, at last, can save us?" The resounding answer of the book of Hebrews is "Christ and Christ alone."

CHAPTER ONE

A Person
Is Worth a Thousand Pictures

Hebrews 1:1-3

During the Second World War, a mother whose husband was overseas fighting in Europe asked her ten-year-old son what he wanted for Christmas. For several minutes, the boy just stared silently at the picture of a uniformed soldier proudly displayed on a nearby desk. Finally he answered, "I wish my father would step out of that frame."[1]

It is the essential message of the gospel that our Heavenly Father has done just that in the incarnation of Jesus Christ—"God was in Christ reconciling the world unto himself" (2 Corinthians 5:19, NASB). In Christ, the portrait has finally become a person. For centuries, God had shown men His profile—His image etched on the face of creation, His will carved on tables of stone, His words echoed in the voices of the prophets. Glimpses, good glimpses, all of them, of the nature and will of God. Manifestations, representations, reasonable facsimiles. But finally, "in these last days," the Word spoken and the Word written has become the Word incarnate.

The Portraits: "God Has Spoken"

The opening statement of the book of Hebrews is the very premise of the Bible: God has communicated with man. The Bible begins with God's word of creation ("Let there be") and concludes with God's word of invitation ("The Spirit and the Bride say come"). It is, from cover to cover, a transcript of God's dialogue with man. From its pages, we are allowed to overhear the very words of God.

---

[1]E. Stanley Jones, *How to Be a Transformed Person* (Nashville: Abingdon, 1978), p. 73.

The Design of God's Speech

The author of Hebrews begins by considering the various means by which God has spoken. But before we ask the question, "How has God spoken?" perhaps we need to ask another question: "Why has God spoken?"

God's speech is His self-expression. Whenever we say something, we say something about ourselves. Our accents tell people where we come from, and our words tell them where we are going. Our vocabularies tell them what we know, and our inflections tell them how we feel. Whether intentionally or unintentionally, purposefully or accidentally, when we speak, we "express ourselves." We disclose our thoughts, convey our opinions, and reveal our inner persons. As the adage puts it, "If you listen to people long enough, they will tell you who they are."

The same is true of the God who has spoken to man. His word on any subject is really a word about himself. His speech is His self-disclosure, revealing His nature and His will to man. God speaks to us because He wants us to know Him—what He is like, how He feels about us, what He wishes for us, and what He desires from us. God has spoken to tell us who He is.

God's speech is His self-extension. Our words activate our thoughts. They extend our private wishes into a public domain where they have the potential to become reality. Words turn emotions into relationships, plans into progress, aspirations into achievements. To a degree, words have their own identities. Once spoken, they stand by themselves. That is the reason it is so hard to "take them back."

If this is true of human speech, it is even more true of God's speech. God speaks with ultimate power and authority. His words go forth from Him with all the force of the sovereign Lord of the universe. They extend His will into His world, and they must be taken seriously. As God affirms through His prophet Isaiah:

> So is my word that goes out from my mouth:
>> It will not return to me empty,
> but will accomplish what I desire
>> and achieve the purpose for which I sent it (Isaiah 55:11).

Not only does God extend himself with His words to accomplish His will, He also extends himself to man with an invitation to fellowship and communion. God does not just speak *to* man, He speaks *with* man. The Bible does not record a monologue, but a dialogue. God not only speaks, He listens. He listens even when the listening is not easy. He listens to complaint as well as to praise. He hears our expressions of fear and well as our expressions of faith. The God who created us converses with us and thereby honors us with an invitation to fellowship. When we hearken to God's communication, we open the door to the possibility of communion with the One who made us in His image and likeness.

The Diversity of God's Speech

The God who has spoken to humanity is a God of many words. The divine-human conversation recorded in Scripture is multidimensional in subject and form. The Biblical transcript of this dialogue supports the affirmation of the author of Hebrews that God has spoken "at many times and in various ways."

God's speech in the Bible is limitless in its forms. If you think that the Bible is just a bunch of *thou shalt not*s and *thus saith*s, then you simply have not read it very well. There is nothing ordinary or predictable about the conversations of God with man in the Scriptures. Quite the contrary, we find God continuously coming to people to tell them just what they need to hear, at just the right time, and in just the right manner.

To recognize this is to understand the significance of some of the more dramatic and unusual ways that God has spoken to humanity. Through the ten plagues and the miracle in the sea, God manipulated nature to teach the Egyptians and the Israelites that the Creator, not the created thing, is the one true God (Exodus 7:5; 12:12). In a midnight wrestling match, God taught Jacob that his life had been more than a struggle with men and that it was not until the "God-striver" (Israel) came to terms with his ultimate Opponent that he would find the destiny for which he had so desperately struggled (Genesis 32:22-32). God opened the lips of a donkey to teach a misguided prophet named Balaam that the Lord, not man, controls the words that His prophets speak (Numbers 22:21-35). In a "still, small voice" God conversed with Elijah to remind him that He was present and active in the lives of His people in forms other than the spectacular and miraculous (1 Kings 19:11-13). To a spiritually unfaithful Israel was sent the prophet Hosea to portray God as a loving husband married to a harlotrous wife whom He still loved and wished to forgive (Hosea 1-3). To a spiritually recalcitrant Israel was sent the prophet Jeremiah to remind them that they were still clay in the potter's hand (Jeremiah 18). To a spiritually thirsty

Israel was sent the prophet Isaiah to offer them the waters that quench eternally (Isaiah 55). "At many times and in various ways. . . ." Quite the conversationalist, this God who speaks to humankind.

God's speech in the Bible is limited in its force. The phrase "at many times and in various ways" describes more than the variety of God's speech in Scripture. It also characterizes the limited nature of God's verbal self-disclosure. This phrase implies that, for all its appropriateness, variety, and power, God's speech through the prophets was yet fragmentary and incomplete—limited and inadequate in its ability to reveal the very essence of God.

This limitation does not grow out of God's inability to reveal himself. It grows out of man's inability to receive that revelation. The difference between God and humans is so great that mere words simply cannot span the gap. As God reminds Israel through the prophet Isaiah:

> "For my thoughts are not your thoughts,
>> neither are your ways my ways," declares the Lord.
> "As the heavens are higher than the earth,
>> so are my ways higher than your ways
>> and my thoughts than your thoughts" (Isaiah 55:8, 9).

To the prophets fell the great challenge of revealing the One who is totally other, ultimately different. It was no easy task. How do you portray the spiritual to the material, the eternal to the temporal? How do you describe the indescribable, comprehend the incomprehensible, express the inexpressible? Just what word do you use for *God*? God is *great,* God is *good.* He is *loving,* He is *terrifying.* He is *merciful,* He is *just.* He is *powerful,* He is *patient. Lord, King, Creator, Savior, Father*—all good words for *God.* But what is *the word* for *God*? Just who is He, and what is He like?

There is something here that is simply beyond words to express. There is no sound human lips can form, no symbol human hands can inscribe to speak adequately of God. We look at His self-portraits on the face of creation and in the pages of Scripture, and, like Saturday spectators in an art museum, we admit to being overawed by it all. We come away with as many questions as we do answers. Just who is this artist? What is He really like? What is He trying to say?

Seeing His handiwork, we want to see His hands. Beholding His art, we want to meet the artist. Like Moses of old, we wish to see the Person behind the portraits. We wish to see God in His glory. We wish to see God "face to face" (Exodus 33:18-23).

The Person: "by His Son"

The Word became flesh and made His dwelling among us. We have seen his glory . . . (John 1:14).

Anyone who has seen me has seen the Father (John 14:9).

If you want to know what God is really like, look closely at Jesus Christ. The author of Hebrews joins a chorus of New Testament witnesses to declare that Jesus of Nazareth is the full and final disclosure of the nature and will of God. What could not be achieved by revelation has been achieved by incarnation. What could not be put into words has been put into flesh. What could not be spoken and could not be written has at last been lived.

The Divinity of God's Son

Jesus is many things to many people. He has been regarded as a great humanitarian and rejected as a hopeless mystic. He has been heralded as social reformer who forever changed the world, and He has been pitied as a misguided fanatic who has no place in the real world. His name is used as a code word to conclude prayers and as an expletive to punctuate profane speech. Some follow Him, some oppose Him, some search for Him, some ignore Him, and some do not know quite what to do with Him.

According to the author of Hebrews, there is only one way to approach Jesus—as the very Son of God. As far as he is concerned, if we have not seen Jesus as the Son, we have not seen Him at all. If we have not received Him as the Son, we have not received Him at all. We must take Him on His terms, or we cannot take Him at all.

The book of Hebrews affirms more than the supremacy of Christ. It affirms the divinity of Christ. Jesus is more than the greatest man. He is the Son of God. He is who God is and He does what God does. The author attributes to the Son the very works of the Father. He made the world, He sustains the world, He purifies the world, He inherits the world, and He presides over the world (Hebrews 1:2, 3). All of the things that define our existence and shape our destiny have come from God through His only Son.

This puts Jesus in a class all by himself. No angel is His equal. No prophet is His peer. With Him no one can compare, no matter how great in stature or how significant in achievements. Not Joshua, not Aaron, not even Moses. Like the Father, the Son is not of the world but is other than the world and over the world. He is, in every way, the incomparable Christ.

The author of Hebrews fights hard for this point because he sees clearly what is at stake. The first and greatest of all sins is the attempt to rob God of His godness, to profane Him by trying to make Him less than He is. To portray God as many (polytheism), to identify Him with some aspect of the material world (animism), or to represent Him by some physical object (idolatry) is to misrepresent His very essence and to assault His sovereignty and His holiness. The tendency of all human religion is to create a smaller, more manageable God who can be controlled and manipulated by man. In the same way that the Old Testament law and the prophets resisted this of God the Father, so also the author of the book of Hebrews resists it of God the Son. He simply will not permit his readers a Jesus who is anything less than the very Son of God. Neither should the church permit it of our generation.

The Disclosure of God Through the Son

When William James was asked to define goodness, he declined but said he could point out a good person. So it is that the Father is revealed through the Son. The prophets revealed God by saying and doing. The Son revealed God by being. The prophets discussed God's power. Jesus demonstrated it. The prophets oracled God's forgiveness. Jesus offered it. The prophets preached God's holiness. Jesus personified it. The prophets spoke of God. Jesus was God in man reconciling the world unto himself.

"The Son is the radiance of God's glory and the exact representation of his being . . ." (Hebrews 1:3). As the sun ray is to the sun, as the impression is to the mold, so is the Son to the Father. Their genetic code is identical, their fingerprints the same. In a mystery that logic simply cannot explain, God the Father and God the Son are one in the same.

"Lord, show us the Father and that will be enough for us" (John 14:8). It was Philip who made the request, but his desire expresses the demand of the modern world. To a whole generation for whom "seeing is believing," Christ's answer is the same one He gave to Philip: "Anyone who has seen me has seen the Father" (John 14:9). So also affirms the author of Hebrews.

Do you yet wish to see God? Do you wish to see His power? See Christ risen from the grave. Do you wish to see God's holiness? Stand in awe of the sinless life of the Son. Do you wish to see His

18

humility? Witness the Christ child in the manger. Do you wish to see His utter love for man? Behold the Christ of Calvary.

The famous ballerina, Anna Pavlova, was once asked to explain the meaning of one of her performances. She replied, "Do you think I would dance it if I could explain it?" There are simply some things that cannot be put into words. So it is with God's self-disclosure to man. What He could not pronounce, He performed—"in these last days he has spoken to us by his Son."

CHAPTER TWO

The Medium or the Message?

Hebrews 1:4—2:18

In the process of communication, there often exists a tension between medium and message. There is a tendency to lose the message in the medium or to allow the medium to become the message. We seem to have a penchant for paying more attention to the speaker than we do to the speech. We notice the musician more than we notice the music, the politician more than the policy, and the preacher more than the preached word. We don't just enjoy good communicators, we virtually enshrine them. We worship at the feet of those who are good with words, and it doesn't much matter whether or not their words are truly good.

Such was the case when the book of Hebrews was written. The Jewish Christians whom the author addressed also had their media idols. Theirs, however, were of the superhuman variety. Instead of pop musicians, talk-show hosts, and television evangelists, their preoccupation was with angels—the supernatural bearers of the word of God. Unfortunately, the attention that they were giving to these "messengers" came at the expense of the attention they should have been giving to the message—God in Christ reconciling the world unto himself. In this portion of the book (Hebrews 1:4—2:18), the author attempts to redirect their misguided interest in angels back to the Christ.

Affirmation: the Message Is Superior to the Messengers

So he became . . . superior to the angels . . . (Hebrews 1:4).

The Greek term from which we get our word *angel* means messenger. Like its Old Testament Hebrew counterpart *(malak)*, this term *(angelos)* is used to describe those who deliver the words of God to men. Though at times the term is used to refer to human messengers, it more often denotes messengers of the superhuman variety. It is obvious, from the amount of attention our author gives to proving the superiority of the Son to angels, that his readers were putting angels on the same level as the Christ. They may have been glorifying angels to a level of divinity. More likely, they were reducing the status of Christ to that of an angel—a superhuman creature sent by God to communicate His will. Either conclusion is in error and represents a serious challenge to the unique status of Christ as the only begotten of the Father, who alone is worthy of honor and praise. For this truth our author now contends by demonstrating that the Son of God is superior to the angels in His relationship to the God who speaks and in His relationship to the people who hear.

The Son Is Superior to the Angels
n His Relationship to the God Who Speaks (1:4-14)

> For to which of the angels did God ever say, "You are my Son . . . "? (Hebrews 1:5).

The quality of communication is often determined by the qualifications of the communicator. No one was ever better qualified to speak for God than His only begotten Son. It was primarily a matter of relationship. "I and the Father are one," Jesus said (John 10:30). The Son knew what the Father knew, He thought what the Father thought, He felt what the Father felt. When He spoke, He truly spoke for the Father.

Here is a qualification the angels simply did not possess. Through a series of seven quotations from the Old Testament, our author draws sharp contrasts between Christ and the angels to prove that they cannot begin to compare to Christ as a communicator of the mind of God. In the same way that the label "prophet" is inadequate for Jesus (Hebrews 1:1-3), so also is the label "angel." The angels are able to speak for God, but Jesus spoke as God. The angels are God's servants, but the Christ is God's Son. The angels are a part of the created order, but the Son is the creator of that order. The angels receive God's commands, but the Son inherits God's throne. Jesus is not to be identified with the angels; He is to worshiped by the angels (Hebrews 1:6).

To mistake Christ for an angel is to mistake the message for the messenger, the Word for those who bear it. It is a confusion that continues to plague Christianity. Christians still mistake the church building for the church, the sacraments for the Savior, the process of worship for the person of worship. Loyalty that belongs to Christ is often pledged to His ministers. Trust that should be placed in Christ is instead placed in the theological systems that attempt to explain Him. Attention that should be focused on Christ is instead focused on polity, programs, and personalities. Like the woman in need of healing (Mark 5:24-34) we seem content to grab for the garments of the Christ instead of meeting the person who gives them the power that we seek.

As Jesus would not permit this of this woman, neither will the author of Hebrews permit it of his readers. He will not let them confuse the message with its media, even the divinely appointed ones. Instead, He forces them to distinguish between the means and the the end of God's self-disclosure to man. It is a distinction we must continue to make. The Bible is divinely appointed, but it does not save. It reveals the Christ who saves. The church is divinely appointed, but it does not save. It calls men and women to the Christ who saves. Baptism is divinely appointed, but it does not save. By it we come into the Christ who saves. Evangelists, elders, and deacons are divinely appointed, but they do not save. They minister to the glory of the Christ who saves.

Ironically, we have allowed some of the means of Christianity to become its end. Instead of using them to glorify the Christ, we allow them to get in the way of the Christ. Instead of employing them to communicate Christ, we allow them to compete with Christ. We identify Christianity with facilities, theologies, methodologies, and personalities instead of identifying it with Christ. In the process, we exalt the form of the gospel at the expense of its substance and rob it of its power to save.

Christianity is not a cathedral, no matter how majestic its architecture or how elegant its appointments. Christianity is not an ecclesiastical body, no matter how sophisticated its organization or how powerful its influence. Christianity is not a preacher, no matter how charismatic his demeanor or how powerful his words. Christianity is a person—the very Son of God sent by the Father to reveal God to man and call man to God. He is not some medium of God's word to man; He *is* God's word to man.

The Son Is Superior to the Angels
n His Relationship with the People Who Hear (2:5-18)

He too shared in their humanity . . . (Hebrews 2:14).

To be an effective communicator, one must know both his message and his audience. As a communicator of the truth of God to man, Jesus was eminently qualified on both grounds. Better than any angel, He knew God's message because He was God's Son. Likewise, better than any angel, He knew His audience because He was God's Son in the flesh.

The humanity of Christ posed a problem for these first-century Christians. It was difficult for them to think of anyone in human flesh as equal even to an angel, much less equal to God. Our author now deals with this issue by pointing out that the glorification of the Son in His incarnation exceeded by far the limitation of the Son in His incarnation. Rather than rob the Son of His divinity, the incarnation actually revealed the Son's divinity in a new and more compelling way. The God above men was now among men, and there was no mistaking who He was. What they before could only vaguely conceptualize, they now could clearly recognize. "We have seen Him," they said. "Our hands have actually touched Him." (See 1 John 1:1, 2.) "We have heard that He is the Lord of nature, but now we have seen Him calm the sea." "We have been taught that He is the Lord of love, but now we have stood beneath His cross." "We have heard He is the Lord of life, but now we kneel before the risen Christ!" What was once believed has now been beheld—"the glory as of the only begotten from the Father" (John 1:14, New American Standard Bible).

The incarnation was about more than the Son's *glorification.* It was also about His *qualification* as messenger of God and Savior of mankind. In a remarkable statement, the author tells us that "it was fitting that God . . . should make the author of their salvation perfect through suffering" (Hebrews 2:10). In what sense does the Son of God need to be "made perfect"? It certainly has nothing to do with His character, for the Son shares the very nature of the Father. It does, however, have something to do with His calling.

It was the Father's will that the Son would save man by becoming man and doing for man what he could not do for himself. The Son would not merely announce man's deliverance, He would achieve it. He would not merely proclaim them liberated from death, He would personally lead them from death to eternal life. The Son is designated the "pathfinder" or the "pioneer" (New International Version: "author"; Greek: *archegos)* of their salvation (Hebrews 12:2). He was being sent to pave a path for man to follow. If men were to follow it, then a man needed to pave it. A man who was a man in every sense of the word. A man capable of disobeying God (He was "tempted," Hebrews 2:18; 4:15). A man confronted by His finitude

("He suffered death," Hebrews 2:9, 14). A man "like his brothers in every way" (Hebrews 2:17).

When Jesus says, "Follow Me," He knows exactly what He is asking. When He calls us to love our enemies, He speaks as one who had enemies. When He calls us to pray that we fall not into temptation, He speaks as one who has been tempted. When He calls us to consider ourselves blessed when persecuted for righteousness' sake, He speaks as one who was so persecuted. When He calls on us to take up our cross and follow Him, He knows exactly where He is asking us to go. He has been there. He came in the flesh, was tempted in the flesh, suffered in the flesh, and conquered the flesh. When He speaks to me, He speaks as one who understands me in every way.

Exhortation: Hearken to the Message of God's Son

> We must pay more careful attention, therefore, to what we have heard (Hebrews 2:1).

Listening is a lost art in this age of the media. In self-defense, we have conditioned ourselves to tune out what we do not want or need to hear. Like a television viewer with remote control in hand, we go quickly from channel to channel in search of that which can make us want to watch and listen. Knowing this, the media moguls manipulate us with a set of sure-fire attention getters: sex, violence, comedy, mystery, and adventure—we'll watch that. Make us lust, make us laugh, make us fear, or make us fantasize, and we will tune in, at least for a while. Eventually, though, we get bored even with these. We fall asleep in front of the set and then awaken to a very empty screen.

In desperation, we spin the dial or press the fast forward in search of something—anything—worth watching or worth hearing. Occasionally, we even pick up a book. And sometimes, we even pick up *the* Book. You know, the one our mothers read, the one the Gideons left. Tired of distractions, we begin to search for direction—a way to go, something worthwhile to do, something worthy to become. Bored with delusions, we look for deliverance—from our emptiness, from our aimlessness, from ourselves. And from the pages of the Book comes a person with a new and different message. One that does not let us run from ourselves, but forces us to confront ourselves. One that honestly shows us what we are and what we should be and provides a way to become it.

God's Message in Christ Delivers Us

This salvation, which was first announced by the Lord (Hebrews 2:3).

Salvation, as a term and as a concept, is passé to most moderns. It recalls the ideals of bygone days and resurrects images of Hellfire and brimstone sermons in tents with sawdust floors, *Jesus Saves* in neon lights atop some church in a city slum, or *Prepare to Meet Thy God* on a faded billboard in the country. It is a vestige of simpler, less sophisticated times when people still sought help from "above."

But now we know better. Our problems are not theological, they are psychological and sociological. Our help cometh from within and from one another. We research ourselves, reorder ourselves, reform ourselves, and rely upon ourselves to fix what is wrong with ourselves. But our anxiety does not go away. We fear and we fret and we still don't know why. "Restless are our hearts," said Augustine. "Restless are our hearts, until they rest in Thee."

Perhaps we had better stay with God a while longer. Perhaps *salvation* is not as outdated as we think. Actually, the term is not nearly as churchy as we have made it. To the people who first heard it, it simply meant "rescue, deliver, preserve." To be "saved" is to be "rescued" or "delivered" *from* something and to be "preserved" *for* something. It is to be rescued from our lusts and delivered from our dishonesty. It is to be rescued from our greed and delivered from our prejudice. It is to be rescued from our hatred, our anger, our arrogance, and our inhumanity to our fellow man. It is to be delivered from our own self-destruction.

To be "saved" is also to be preserved—preserved for giving, for serving, for forgiving, for healing, for encouraging, and for loving in every way. It is to be preserved for a destiny—the one for which we were created and have so cheaply forfeited, now reclaimed for us by the Son of God. To be saved is to be delivered from death and preserved for life in its finest and fullest sense.

God's Message in Christ Makes Demands of Us

How shall we escape if we ignore such a great salvation? (Hebrews 2:3).

Here, at last, is a message that deserves—no, demands—a hearing. This is no take-it-or-leave-it matter. God has become man in His Son, Jesus Christ. He died in our place so we would not have to pay the penalty for our sins. He rose again from the grave to deliver us from death and to grant us eternal life. We can't ignore this. We can't sweep it under some historical rug and pretend that it never happened. We can't cover it up with theological gibberish and make of it something other than what it really was. This is the most important thing that ever happened, the greatest thing that God has ever done. We can't run from this. We can't avoid it. God won't let us. Having made us aware of Him, He now makes us accountable to Him. The God who created us by the Son and saved us through the Son is now calling us in the Son, and He demands an answer. On that answer hang our eternal destinies.

A parish priest once came upon a gang of boys who were trashing a cathedral. They went from pew to pew throwing hymnals, scattering prayer books, and shouting obscenities. He startled them with his sudden presence and then proceeded to do a most remarkable thing. Without making a single comment about their behavior, he quietly took a lantern and led them before a large crucifix. Holding the light to it he said, "Now you take a good look at this and then tell me you don't give a damn." For the first time in their lives, they saw Christianity for what it really was. They simply could not treat it lightly anymore.

And so on rude timbers raised against an angry sky hangs the very Son of God. Like never before, we see God for who He really is—how deep His love for us, how rich His mercy toward us, how firm His commitment to us—and we cannot casually dismiss Him. We can ignore a concept, reject a religion, take or leave a theology, but what are we going to do with this God who "so loved the world . . ."?

CHAPTER THREE

Heritage Christian Church

Hebrews 3:1-6

I once preached in a church confronted by a most difficult decision. It was a lovely white frame chapel nestled in a tree-lined meadow—a portrait of tradition just waiting to be painted. Weathered stones jutted up from the lawn surrounding the sanctuary to honor the patron saints of bygone days. "Beloved pastor," "devoted elder," "honored member," read the epitaphs—priceless memories scratched in marble. This church had a lot of dead members!

On any given Sunday, those resting in peace far outnumbered those resting in the pews. It seems that everybody who was anybody in this church was, or wished to be, buried beside it. So great was the demand for a parcel of holy ground that the entire church yard had become a cemetery—a field of stones surrounding a sanctuary with the church steeple presiding as the chief memorial.

Now a new preacher had come to the church—a young man, fresh out of seminary and full of idealism. More interested in the church's future than with its past, he led with vision and preached with fervor and conviction. Well, the church in the cemetery sprang to life. Old members were revived, new members were added, and in the span of a few months the congregation had outgrown its facilities. Further growth would require an expansion of the church plant, but the surrounding cemetery made this impossible. The remaining options were clear but troubling, forcing the little congregation to wrestle with its very identity and sense of purpose. They could simply stay where they were and continue to honor the past, perpetuating the memory of what they used to be, or they could relocate, move on to a new place with a new purpose in search of what they might become. It was a hard choice for Heritage Christian Church.

The Jewish Christians addressed in the book of Hebrews faced a similar dilemma. They, too, were the possessors of a great heritage and they, too, were confronted by the prospect of an even greater destiny. And now they must choose between the two. Their "house" (household) of faith had been built by the greatest of saints—Moses, the man of God. It had served them well for centuries—a rallying point in times of national crisis, a leavening influence in their daily lives, a secure refuge in the face of life's crushing blows. It touched their lives at those points that matter most—childbirth, circumcision, confirmation, marriage, sickness, loss, and death. When everything else had been taken from them, they still had their religion. They rested in that; they found a sense of identity and purpose in it. In a very real sense, Israel was its religion.

But a new man of God had appeared. A man conversant with the traditions but not a slave to them. He spoke as one having His own authority. Born into Judaism, He urged men to live beyond it. Born under the law, He called men to live above it. "The kingdom of God is at hand," He said. "What the prophets predicted is being fulfilled in your day." "The Son of Man has come to seek and save the lost." "Whosoever believes in the Son has eternal life."

Suddenly, the old religion and the old ways were no longer enough. They knew there was something greater here, something superior, some One they must pursue. But at what expense? Must they break with their past to realize their promise? Could they not hold on to the one and reach for the other? Could they not follow both Moses and Christ? Sensitive to their dilemma, the author of this letter gently, but firmly, urges the Hebrews on to the inevitable and necessary decision, calling them to "fix their thoughts upon Jesus."

The Past: the House That Moses Built

Moses was faithful in all God's house (Hebrews 3:2).

To the modern reader, the point that our author now argues—that Jesus is superior to Moses—seems anticlimactic and out of place. After all, had he not just finished proving that the Son was greater than the angels? What more could be gained by showing Him to be superior to a mere mortal? The answer lies in the fact that, to these Jewish Christians, Moses was no "mere mortal."

They Were Honored by Their Past

In the cemetery of Judaism, one headstone stood far above all of the others. It honored the man who was most responsible for Israel's national religion. He wrote down its laws, initiated its institutions, and presided over its infancy. He led its earliest citizens out of slavery to become a free and independent nation in the promised land. He was their patron saint and their founding father all wrapped up into one. In Israel, he had no peer—the man Moses.

The author of Hebrews does not challenge the greatness of Moses. He celebrates it. The very text he quotes, Numbers 12:7, constitutes God's own affirmation of Moses' uniqueness among the prophets: "Moses was faithful in all God's house" (Hebrews 3:2). In the face of a challenge to Moses' prophetic authority, God affirmed Moses as the only one with whom He spoke "face to face" (Numbers 12:1-9; cf. Exodus 33:9-11). Moses was the first to learn the personal name of Israel's God (Exodus 6:2, 3). He alone had been permitted to see even a portion of God's glory (Exodus 33:18-23).

When God threatened to punish Israel for their rebellion, it was Moses who personally pleaded their case before the Lord (Exodus 32:30-35; Numbers 14:10-23). Moses recorded Israel's first laws, anointed Israel's first priests, oversaw the erection of their first sanctuary, instituted their first national worship, organized their first army, and functioned as the first justice of their supreme court. He is designated the prototype of all true prophets and even of the Messiah (Deuteronomy 18:18, 19; cf. Acts 3:20-26). Leader, lawgiver, prophet, preacher, teacher, intercessor—whatever task God assigned him—Moses was "faithful in all God's house."

Moses' accomplishments far outlived him. The religion he helped to found continued to shape the very fabric of Israelite society well into the Christian era. Israel was not known for its government, its military accomplishments, or its economy. It was known for its religion. Its chief export was a spiritual truth, a revolutionary concept that even today continues to shape the faith of three major world religions (Judaism, Islam, and Christianity). "Hear, O Israel: The Lord our God, the Lord is one. Love the Lord your God with all your heart and with all your soul and with all your strength" (Deuteronomy 6:4, 5). That was their creed, what they stood for, who they were. They were proud of that, and rightly so. It was the greatest truth that had ever been revealed to man, and God had chosen to reveal it to Israel.

They Were Hindered by Their Past

The problem with a glorious past is that it often keeps us from moving on into the future. We have a penchant for preserving what has been at the expense of pursuing what should be. Every great

31

spiritual movement is eventually beset by a spiritual nostalgia that tends to venerate the "faith of the fathers," pronounce it normative, and "visit it upon the sons to the third and fourth generations." Therein, lies the dynamic behind the various "-isms" and -ites" that sadly divide Christendom and hinder the fulfillment of its mission.

Knowing what modern Christians have done with Luther, Calvin, and Campbell, it is not difficult to understand what these early Jewish Christians were doing with Moses. They simply could not let him rest in peace. Determined to perpetuate his greatness, they fashioned him into a rigid theological system and put that on a pedestal to preside over their spiritual experience. The result was Judaism, the religion of Israel when Christianity was born, the religion that had helped prepare the world for the coming of Christ. It was what these Jewish Christians once were. Ironically, it now stood in the way of what they must become.

The Promise: the House That Christ Is Building

> But Christ is faithful as a son over God's house. And we are his house, if we hold on to our courage and the hope of which we boast (Hebrews 3:6).

When these Israelites welcomed Christ into their family, they outgrew their old house and moved on to a new one. It was not an easy move. They gave up the proven for the promised and the familiar for the foreseen; but now some of them were having second thoughts. Shunned and even persecuted by those who remained in the house that Moses built, they were having difficulty settling into the house that Christ was building. Our author welcomes them to their new neighborhood with words of encouragement, explaining the benefits and responsibilities of living in a Christ-built home.

The Heavenly Character of Their Promise

When these Jewish converts moved into the house Christ was building, they "moved up"—way up. They now shared in what our author designates as a "heavenly calling" (Hebrews 3:1). To live at that address means at least two things. First, it means to live "apart"—not from the world's people, but from the world's sin. *Heavenly,* as opposed to *worldly,* refers to the life-style of those whom our author calls "holy" (set apart). Second, it means to live "above"—to seek a destiny that reaches beyond the dimensions and dynamics of the material world. It means to live as a citizen of a spiritual kingdom, a child of eternity whose values, loyalties, goals, and affections are not set upon the things of this world, but upon a higher land. Our forwarding address is a residence God has personally prepared (Hebrews 11:16), "the heavenly Jerusalem, the city of the living God" (Hebrews 12:22).

The Human Conditions of Their Promise

If is the biggest little word in our language. It qualifies the possible and places conditions on the promised. It defines the means by which the potential becomes the actual. Our author consistently attaches it to the spiritual prospects of the Hebrew Christians. "And we are his house, if we hold on to our courage and the hope of which we boast" (Hebrews 3:6). The conditionality of this language is undeniable. Those looking for "eternal security" in the book of Hebrews are going to be frustrated by their search. In this book, the "final perseverance of the saints" is offered to saints who persevere. In a fashion consistent with Old Testament covenant theology, our author insists that the promises of God are conditional—fully enjoyed only by those whose faith is manifested in faithfulness. As "Moses was faithful as a servant in all God's house" and "Christ is faithful as a son over God's house," so must Christ's followers be found faithful in God's house (Hebrews 3:5, 6).

For these Hebrew Christians, as it does for us, this meant fixing their thoughts on Jesus and holding on to the hope they had in Him. The faithfulness to which our author calls them is not the pursuit of moral perfection, it is the pursuit of Christ. It is a fascination with Him, a fixation upon Him, a faith in Him as our only hope of salvation. Determined to release them from the prison of the past, the author tries to convince these Jewish converts that Christ is superior to Moses as one who represents God to man (apostle) and as one who represents man to God (high priest). The household Moses founded only prepared for and was superseded by the household of Jesus Christ. Their destiny did not lie in a glorious past but in God's promise. They who had once followed God's servant must now follow God's Son.

The lessons for the church today are obvious. The church that marries itself to one age becomes the widow of the next. Witness the cathedrals of England and Europe, where sanctuaries honoring the living God have been turned into shrines honoring dead men. The church cemetery has been moved from the church yard into the church house, turning the meeting place into a mausoleum. This form of traditional religion has contributed to a spiritual climate in England and Europe that many refer to as the "post-Christian" age.

Christianity is not a religion of patron saints. It is a religion of the personal Savior. The "faith of the fathers" was just that. It was their faith, suitable for their generation. It cannot be canonized and made normative for their descendants. Though the truths upon which it was founded are fixed and immutable, these truths must be freshly proclaimed and personally embraced by each new generation. As Catherine Marshall put it, "God has no grandsons, only sons."

By the way, Heritage Christian Church decided not to relocate. I have not heard anything from them in recent years. Seems no one else has, either.

CHAPTER FOUR

Conjugating Christianity

Hebrews 3:7—4:11

Christianity is not a noun. It is a verb. It is about what God has done, is doing, and shall do. It is about what we were, are, and shall be. Christianity believes, it hopes, it loves. Christianity cares, it serves, it gives. It is much more than an institution; it is action, a state of being.

The predicate of *faith* can be conjugated in at least three tenses. It is a religion of the past tense, an "old-time" religion of what was and what has been. It is about tradition and precedent, remembering and rehearsing the mighty deeds of God. It is a religion of the future tense, a "pie-in-the-sky" religion of what shall be. It is about prediction and fulfillment, awaiting and anticipating the promises of God. It is also a religion of the present tense, a "here and now" religion of what is. It is about conviction and conduct, believing and behaving in response to God's call.

In the text before us, the author explores the three tenses of the Christian religion with these Jewish converts. The passage is punctuated with a repeated quotation of Psalm 95:7—"Today, if you hear his voice, do not harden your hearts" (Hebrews 3:7, 15; 4:7)—by which he urges these beleaguered Christians to live for today in light of the lessons of the past and the promises of the future.

Learning From the Past—the Rebellion of God's People

Do not harden your hearts as you did in the rebellion (Hebrews 3:8).

Everyone comes to Christ out of the "past." Now a past is a hard thing to shake. It is something you are always trying to live up to or to live down. Some people are proud of their pasts, but most of us are prisoners to them. We are haunted by our pasts, hounded by them—the time we gave in . . . sold out . . . ran away. The thing we should have done but didn't. The place where we should have been but weren't. The habit we should have conquered but couldn't. You can run from the past or you can live in the past, but you can never truly forget the past.

Maybe we should not even try to forget it. The baggage of bygone days can be a blessing as well as a burden. Since we cannot fully leave it behind, perhaps we can, at least, learn from it.

That is exactly what the writer of Hebrews is trying to get these Jewish Christians to do. Essentially, what he says is this: "Remember the past, even regret the past, but—whatever you do—do not repeat the past. You are your father's sons, but you do not need to practice your father's sins."

The "sins of the fathers" upon which he focuses are two: disbelief (Hebrews 3:19; 4:2) and disobedience (Hebrews 3:18; 4:6, 11). They are the primary ingredients in "rebellion" (3:8, 16), and they always travel in pairs. The example he cites was the occasion when the Israelites of the Exodus rejected God's call to enter the promised land. (See Numbers 14.) They did not obey that call because they did not believe the promises of the one who called. As a result, they forfeited their opportunity to enter God's rest.

It was a perfect model for the situation confronting these Hebrew Christians. Before them lay the promise of their own spiritual "land of milk and honey," but in their way stood the "giants" of fear and doubt. Like their fathers, they were on the verge of forfeiting their destiny through disbelief in and disobedience to the "gospel preached to them." By doubting God's promises, they were in danger of missing God's rest.

It is said that those who do not know history are doomed to repeat it. Yet I have observed that even those who do know history seem doomed to repeat it. "Their hearts are always going astray," said God of that rebellious generation. He said it as if with shrugged shoulders and an open-palmed, incredulous sigh (Hebrews 3:10). Surely He must still be sighing. Stubbornly, we continue to test God's justice and try His patience (cf. Hebrews 3:9). With little or no appreciation of the lessons of the past, we barge into the future along the same dead-end streets of our predecessors. We go where they went, do what they did, and pay the same price. You would think we would learn.

"History repeats itself," someone has said. Seems that it has to. Nobody listens! For the Christian, the past is not something to live in. It is something to learn from. It is when we are most sensitive to history that we are most capable of making history. More than just a reservoir of what we were, the past can be a resource for what we are to become.

Longing for the Future—the Rest for God's People

There remains . . . a Sabbath-rest for the people of God (Hebrews 4:9).

There is a sense in which Christianity is a future tense religion—a religion of "pie in the sky" and "the sweet by and by." Though critics often scoff at this tense of our faith as cowardly escapism or just so much sentimental tripe, there is nothing more basic to Biblical Christianity than what it hopes for—the hereafter. The second coming, Heaven, Hell, punishment, reward—all are major tenets of a faith that preaches, "This world is not my home." *Believe* and *hope* are future tense verbs. Christians await, they expect, they anticipate what is to come.

The expectation our author sets before the Hebrew Christians is one of the most inviting promises of the New Testament—rest. The prospect of a "Sabbath-rest" in Canaan, which their forefathers had never fully enjoyed, is now offered to them, if they are willing to enter into it by an obedient faith (Hebrews 4:1-11). The "rest" of which he speaks is the rest that God himself has enjoyed since the completion of His creation (Hebrews 4:10). This "Sabbath" not only commemorates the end of God's work of creation; it also anticipates the end of our work toward spiritual maturation.

If there was anything these beleaguered Christians needed, it was rest. For them, Christianity had been work—hard work. As we noted in the introduction, the Hebrew Christians had been forced to pay a price for their conversion. Their discipleship had come at the cost of public ridicule, confiscation of personal property and, for some, imprisonment (Hebrews 10:32-34). All of this had taken its toll. It had left them tired, the worst kind of tired—tired of struggling against a foe that will not go away, tired of wrestling with problems that seem to have no solution. It was the kind of fatigue that Julia Ward Howe once described as "tired way down into the future."

This kind of fatigue can do strange things to us. It acts like a drug: it dulls the mind, weakens the will, and diminishes our resolve. As Vince Lombardi once put it, "Fatigue makes cowards of us all." This kind of tiredness can affect a whole generation. It gets into the stuff of the mind, spreads like an epidemic, and becomes the prevailing mood of an age. It was true of that generation of their forefathers who got lost somewhere in the wilderness. Maybe it was the long years of slavery in Egypt, or perhaps it was the monotonous insecurity of the desert. But something had bleached the fight right out of them. They got tired quickly and were easily disheartened. They met problems with panic and obstacles with an ornery murmur. Their dreams began to darken into doubts—doubts about Moses, about the promised land, and, most seriously, about the power of God. Fatigue deteriorated into faithlessness, and they fell along the way. The writer sets this tragic model of unrealized rest before these tired Christians and then urges them to "make every effort to enter that rest," which their forefathers never enjoyed (Hebrews 4:11).

The rest God promises is rest *from* labor (Hebrews 4:10). True rest always is. Rest *instead of* work is really no rest at all. It is escape, irresponsibility, unfaithfulness. Those who seek this kind of rest never find their way out of the wilderness. By contrast, rest *from* work suggests devotion and commitment. It is about accomplishment and fulfillment—the satisfaction of having expended effort towards the completion of some worthwhile task.

God's children still seek this kind of rest. There are some things we never quite finish this side of Canaan. We sow seeds of love in a hungry land and the weeds of hatred and indifference spring up to deny the harvest. We light lamps of brotherhood and understanding only to watch the cold winds of prejudice stir up to put them out. We strive to build our own Christian characters only to be frustrated at every turn. It is like trying to build a castle of sand on the shore of a pounding surf. Just about the time we put the finishing touches on our fortress of piety, a new wave of temptation washes it all away.

Like fumbling apprentices, we also continue to work on our faith. We put in overtime trying to reconcile it to life. We struggle with the unfair tragedies that seem to contradict God's goodness. We wrestle with recurring feelings of guilt that seem to invalidate His forgiveness. Our strength is sapped by stubborn anxieties that impede His peace. After a while, we quietly begin to wonder whether there will ever be an end to this doubt-filled "process without progress."

But the divine foreman who supervises this great spiritual enterprise looks down on our efforts to offer a great promise—"You will rest from your labor." The unfinished tasks will be completed. The never-ending struggles will come to an end. We will leave them in the wilderness to enter our promised land. For the final time, we will at last lay down the tools of our trade to rest with the satisfaction of knowing that the great work He has begun in us has finally been completed (Philippians 1:6).

There is an end to the career of faith—an end of finished work, fulfilled hope, and a realized destiny. The future tense of Christianity is "future perfect" in every way.

Living in the Present—the Response of God's People

> We have come to share in Christ if we hold firmly till the end the confidence we had at first (Hebrews 3:14).

A wise pastor once responded to a bitter woman's resentful cry with a statement that captures the essence of Christianity as a present tense religion. Angry at God over what had happened in her life, she defiantly protested, "I wish I had never been made!" To this ingratitude, the pastor replied, "You haven't been made. You are still being made."

So it is in the Christian life. There is an existential dimension to our faith. There is a sense in which we are ever becoming Christian. In fact, the moment we begin to think we have become Christian is the very moment we begin to unbecome Christian. God is concerned about more than what we have done for Him. He is concerned about what we have done for Him lately. "Today," insists our author, "Today, if you hear his voice, do not harden your hearts" (Hebrews 3:7, 15; 4:7). God simply refuses to leave us alone. It is as if He keeps His finger on our spiritual pulse. He will not let us rest on our laurels or bide our time. Instead, He continually confronts us with some moment of truth to which we must respond.

Simply stated, the responses God seeks from us are two, the combination of which the Bible calls "faithfulness": faith and obedience. So much for "simply stated." There is nothing simple about these concepts, including how they relate to one another. Some theologies insist these responses are in tension. Here they are in tandem. Faith and obedience are the two legs upon which Christianity stands, the two oars that propel our boat of salvation. If you try to stand on only one, you are sure to fall, and if you try to row with only one, you are sure to get nowhere.

These concepts are so closely related in the mind of our author that he uses them interchangeably in this portion of his letter. Why was it that the generation that left Egypt never made it to the promised land? It was because they "disobeyed" (Greek, *apeitheo*), he answers in Hebrews 3:18 (cf. also Hebrews 4:6, 11). Yet, in the very next verse, he says they failed to reach that land because of their "unbelief" (*apistia*).

39

So which was it? Both! One cannot be separated from the other because one grows out of the other. In other words, they disobeyed because they disbelieved. Conversely, obedience, which is about conduct, grows out of faith, which is about conviction, and together they constitute faithfulness. Simply stated (there's that expression again!), faithfulness is behavior consistent with belief. It is remaining true to one's convictions.

The same terms are used in John the Baptist's testimony about the two responses one can make to Jesus Christ: "Whoever believes (Greek, *pisteuo*) in the Son has eternal life, but whoever rejects (*apeitheo*) the Son will not see life, for God's wrath remains on him" (John 3:36). John means the same thing by *rejects* that the author of Hebrews means by *disobeys*. The "disobedience" of which he speaks is not some occasional slip-up in personal morality, some uncharacteristic breach of a commandment. It is refusal to follow God or, as our author states it, "turn[ing] away from the living God" (Hebrews 3:12). This is the essence of what that generation in the wilderness did when they refused to enter Canaan. It is what the Hebrew Christians are in danger of doing if they refuse to follow Christ. The faithfulness he calls forth from them is that of holding firmly till the end the "confidence" (assurance, conviction) they had at first (Hebrews 3:14).

Believe and *obey* are present tense verbs. They are what we do between Egypt and Canaan, in the wilderness that lies between redemption and final rest. For somewhere along the way, God will come calling. After the desert has taken its toll and the manna no longer satisfies, when our drive has deserted us and our dreams begin to fade, He will come calling. He will expect us to finish what we have started, to go on to Canaan. As He confronted these ancient Israelites, He will confront us with a choice, a moment of truth. Do we really believe in God's promises? Are we willing to bet our lives on them?

The call comes to break camp one final time. Instinctively, we reach again for the tent peg as we have done a thousand times before. But this time, our doubts get in the way. You see there's this rumor in the camp that there may not be anything all that special beyond this wilderness, or, if there is, that we cannot attain it. Even the experts whom we trust to tell us about what lies "beyond" are divided in their opinion. Some say it's great, this land beyond the river, and it is ours for the taking. Others are not so sure. In fact, the majority opinion is that there is really nothing "over there," at least, nothing for us. They say this whole miserable journey has been nothing but a cruel joke—and we are the punch line. We gave up the security of Egypt for the sacrifices of the wilderness, and for what? A grave, that's what!

Suddenly, we are struck by a panic-inducing thought. Maybe our entire lives, all that we have stood for, all that we have tried to be and do has been a waste—a sad, cruel waste. Maybe we are going to die without really having lived. Maybe we have missed this life while in search of a better one. All that we have denied ourselves, all that we pushed ourselves so hard to achieve, maybe it has come to nothing. Maybe we ought just to turn around and go back—back to Egypt, back to security, back to slavery.

Our thoughts are interrupted by a voice. It is a familiar voice, a confident voice, a strong, compelling voice. It is the voice that said, "Leave Egypt. . . . Follow Me. . . . I am the Lord your God." And now it calls us to "go on over into Canaan." Suddenly, what we think and what other people are saying is no longer important. What is important is that voice. Fear gives way to faith, and doubt to determination. Somehow we muster the courage to move on. Yesterday was almost more than we could bear, and tomorrow—well, who knows for sure what it holds. But today—today—we hear His voice, and we will not harden our hearts!

CHAPTER FIVE

The Naked Christian

Hebrews 4:12, 13

The Emperor's New Clothes is a classic fairy tale by Hans Christian Andersen. It is about a pompous king whose vanity and passion for clothes is exploited by swindlers to their profit and to his embarrassment. These "gentlemen weavers" convince the king that, for a handsome price, they can produce a garment of such exquisite beauty that it can be appreciated only by the wise and capable. To the unqualified and the ignorant, it is completely invisible! The money changes hands, and the king is enthralled by the prospect of wearing clothes that can both compliment him and expose the incompetence of his subjects.

One by one, the king's ministers are sent to inquire of the weavers' progress. Though not a single one of them can actually see the nonexistent garment, they praise it anyway for fear of being labeled foolish and pronounced unfit for their posts. Finally, the king himself goes to examine the garment and, though seeing nothing, yet praises it out of fear that he, too, will be called a fool. The climax of the story has the king walking stark naked through the town, pretending to wear garments that do not exist, to the cheers of the people who pretend to see them. The farce is rudely interrupted by a little child who calls attention to the obvious fact that everybody, including the king, is finally forced to admit: "He has nothing on!" The tale ends with the king bravely pronouncing that "the procession must go on." Pretending to wear a robe that does not exist, he stiffly continues along the path of the procession followed by chamberlains who hold up an invisible train.

The tale, of course, is a parody of pretense, a satire on the self-delusion of human vanity and pride—an affliction common to more than kings (or so I am told). The irony of the story lies in the fact that the garment, which was itself a lie but which promised to "distinguish the wise men from the fools," does just that. It exposes the foolishness of pretension, the farce of trying to save face at the expense of the truth.

Here, at last, is where the fairy tale crosses paths with our text. I do not know whether Hans Christian Andersen ever read Hebrews 4:12 and 13, but his story certainly echoes its message. It is foolish to pretend, to clothe ourselves with insincerity, to represent ourselves as something other than what we really are. It is foolish because we simply will not get away with it. Sooner or later, we will be exposed. The author reminds us, as he does these Hebrew Christians, that we live our lives not just before the eyes of men, but "before the eyes of him to whom we must give account" (Hebrews 4:13). He sobers us with the the assertion that we will someday stand completely naked before a God who sees us, not as we pretend to be, but as we really are.

Exposed by God

> Nothing in all creation is hidden from God's sight. Everything is uncovered and laid bare (Hebrews 4:13).

The first thing that Adam and Eve did after they ate of the forbidden fruit was to hide. They hid from each other and they hid from God. In so doing, they personify fallen humankind. The tragic sequence is repeated with every sin. Rebellion is followed by guilt, guilt by fear, fear by pretense. According to the Bible, we hide because we sin.

Some people spend all their days hiding. Their lives are nothing but a charade, a great hypocrisy. Eventually they become prisoners to their pretense, resorting continually to fabrication and delusion in order to conceal the persons they really are. They are so preoccupied with hiding themselves that they end up losing themselves; they forfeit their true identity.

They are much like the woman of whom Helen Joseph writes in her poem, "The Mask":

Always a mask
Held in the slim hand,
Whitely,
Always she had a mask
Before her face—
Smiling and sprightly,
The Mask.

Truly the wrist
Holding it lightly
Fitted the task:
Sometimes however
Was there a shiver,
Fingertip quiver,
Ever so slightly—
Holding the mask?

For years and years and
Years I wondered
But dared not ask.
And then—
I blundered
I looked behind,
Behind the mask
To find
Nothing—
She had no face
She had become
Merely a hand
Holding a mask
With grace.

Our masks may conceal us from others, but they simply cannot conceal us from God. He sees through them and looks behind them, determined to deal with the real person. From Him there is nothing hidden. Before Him all things are uncovered and open. God "finds us out." As the apostle Paul says in 1 Corinthians 4:5, "He will bring to light what is hidden in darkness and will expose the motives of men's hearts."

According to our text, the instrument of this divine exposé of man is the living and active word of God. Here, "the word of God" refers not to the eternal *logos* who became flesh in Jesus of Nazareth (John 1), but to the authoritative commands of God that demand obedience of men. Like sharp daggers, God's commands pierce our pretensions to disclose our true level of trust and commitment. By insisting that we act on our faith, God's commands reveal our faith or lack of it. As Jesus put it, "Why do you call me, 'Lord, Lord,' and do not do what I say?" (Luke 6:46). The "double-edged sword" not only reveals God to man, it also reveals man to God.

... before the eyes of him to whom we must give account (Hebrews 4:13).

It is no wonder that modern man has difficulty believing in a God "to whom we must give account." Culturally conditioned to be "under no obligation," we spend most of our lives running from responsibility and resisting any and all efforts to hold us accountable. Determined to "owe no man," we build loopholes into our laws and put escape clauses into our contracts. We get out of bad debts by filing for bankruptcy, and we get out of bad marriages by filing for divorce. We resent other people's telling us how to run our lives, and we refuse to be bound by any standard other than our own. To a world that seeks to answer to no man, the prospect of having to answer to God is a thought from which we steadfastly recoil.

But, whether we like it or not, the God of the Bible is a God who judges His creatures. The God of creation is also the God of the flood. The shepherd who lays down His life for His sheep is also the shepherd who will separate the sheep from the goats. No portrait of God is complete that does not recognize His determination to hold men accountable. He is the sovereign who scrutinizes His subjects both in this life and at the end of it.

This scrutinizing sovereign has X-ray eyes. His examination of us is the spiritual equivalent of exploratory surgery. His razor-sharp scalpel penetrates to the inner man to expose "the thoughts and attitudes of the heart" (Hebrews 4:12). In other words, God's diagnosis of our sinful symptoms reaches beyond what we say and do to what we think and feel. This supernatural surgeon practices internal medicine. His specialty is cardiology. He is a God who "looks at the heart" (1 Samuel 16:7) and who knows the heart of everyone (Acts 1:24; 15:8).

The reasons that God focuses His diagnostic tests upon our hearts are probably two. First, according to the Bible, the "heart" is the seat of human intellect and will. It is that part of us that dreams and schemes, that plans and decides. It is, therefore, the source of human behavior. Second, a man's heart does not always match a man's habits. What a man does is not always consistent with what he really wishes to do. It is the motive behind the behavior that best defines the meaning of the behavior. It is only when we know the heart behind the habit that we know the real person.

This explains God's special interest in the hearts of men. We see it all through Scripture. *Thou shalt not covet* dictates the tenth and final commandment. With that prohibition, God extends His authority beyond the actions of men into their hearts in an attempt to temper the motive behind a whole host of misbehaviors (Exodus 20:17). Not just "murder," but "anger"; not just "adultery," but "lust," insists Jesus, are subject to God's judgment (Matthew 5:21, 22, 27, 28). The hearts of men both determine and define the actions of men and, hence, make us what we are. They are, therefore, what God both exposes and examines.

We, like the Hebrew Christians, are thus confronted with a sobering realization. The God who judges us knows us—the real us, not the persons we pretend to be, but who we really are. We cannot fool Him; we cannot hide from Him. We stand totally naked before Him, stripped of every facade and every pretense, completely vulnerable to His scrutiny. "Everything is uncovered and laid bare before the eyes of him to whom we must give account" (Hebrews 4:13).

To be sure, the mere thought of being exposed for who we really are is enough to frighten us. And so our author has intended it. There is a sense in which this text is a warning—a warning against pretending to follow God's Son when our hearts are not really in it. But there is also a sense in which this text is an invitation—an invitation to genuine faith and to true discipleship. As such, it is a positive encouragement to faithfulness. As any recovering alcoholic will tell you, the first step to recovery is the honest admission of the problem. This is likewise true in our efforts to conquer our tendencies toward apostasy. To be successful, we must begin by dealing with our real selves rather than with the poor substitutes we parade before others (and God). Being exposed can be a painful experience, but it can also be a redemptive experience. It peels away the layers of pretense behind which we hide, and it enables us to present our true selves unto God.

In the third book of the C. S. Lewis fantasy, *Chronicles of Narnia*, the character Eustace, along with his companions, sails the *Dawn Treader* to the "very end of the world." Along the way, Eustace stumbles into a dragon's lair and, after "sleeping on a dragon's hoard with greedy, dragonish thoughts," awakens to discover that he has become a dragon himself. He later relates to his friend Edmund how it was that he "stopped being one." A huge lion (the Christ-figure in the *Chronicles*) had approached him and offered him a cure—a bath in a deep well. Only first, he must "undress." Three times Eustace pulled off his dragon's skin only to find another dragon layer beneath it. "You will have to let me undress you," insisted the lion. With great fear, Eustace endured the pain of the lion's claw as it tore the final layer away. Exposed, smooth, and soft, and "smaller than he had been," Eustace was plunged by the lion into the water, from which he emerged "a boy again." Having successfully been "undragoned," he was then clothed by the lion who had stripped him bare, and set free to continue on his journey to the end of the world.

This portrait of regeneration is close to the one presented in Scripture, and illustrates an important implication of this text in Hebrews. Before we can be redeemed, we must be revealed. We must expose ourselves in order to become ourselves—our real selves. Before we can be clothed with the righteousness of Christ, we must be stripped of all pretense. Our motives must be undressed, our attitudes uncovered, our convictions and attitudes "laid bare." As we are born naked, we must be reborn naked, totally exposed by the word of that One "to whom we must give account."

CHAPTER SIX

The Protocol of Salvation

Hebrews 4:14—5:10

Protocol is a term used in military and diplomatic circles to describe the proper procedure for approaching people of rank. It is also used to describe the person who facilitates the process. A protocol is someone who enables access of superiors by subordinates. He intercedes for the subordinate to represent his interests before someone of higher rank. If desirable he will arrange a meeting between the two, properly introduce them, and preside over the conference to see that the request of the subordinate is communicated in a way that shows proper respect for the privacy and privilege of the person of rank. More than mere formality, protocol is the essential format by which important business is conducted in authoritative circles.

According to the Bible, there is also a protocol of salvation. There is a procedure and a person to facilitate our access to the One of ultimate rank. In the Old Testament the procedure was one of sacrifice, offering, and intercessory prayer. The person who presided over it all was the priest. The priest ministered before the Lord's altar at the tent of meeting (where God meets man), to oversee the presentation of offerings and sacrifices and to voice prayers on behalf of the people. His function, not unlike that of a modern protocol, was to assist men in their efforts to come before their Sovereign in a way that did not compromise their Sovereign. It was his duty to help men seek redemption from God while maintaining their reverence for God (cf. Leviticus 10:3).

Knowing the importance of the high priest to the former religion of these Jewish converts, the author of Hebrews now pursues a final point of comparison between Judaism and Christianity that will occupy the remainder of the doctrinal portion of his work (4:14—10:18) and forever stand as his unique contribution to New Testament christology. Using Psalm 110:4 as his starting place and Melchizedek as his model, he boldly proclaims that "Jesus the Son of God," in a manner far superior to his Levitical predecessors, is the "great high priest" who enables us to "approach the throne of grace with confidence, so that we may receive mercy and find grace to help us in our time of need" (Hebrews 4:14, 16; cf. also 10:21-22). Jesus is our key to Heaven's gate, our means of access to God's throne of grace. He is our Protocol of salvation.

Christ's effectiveness as a mediator (connecting link) between man and God stems from two very distinct qualifications that He uniquely possesses for His priestly office. As God in the flesh, He was both fully sympathetic with man and completely subject unto God. Our Protocol knows precisely what we need from our Sovereign and has the full confidence of the One before whose throne He stands.

Our Protocol Is Sympathetic With Man

> For we do not have a high priest who is unable to sympathize with our weaknesses . . . (Hebrews 4:15).

In his poem "The Preacher's Mistake," Brewer Mattocks addresses a shortcoming of many clerics:

The parish priest of austerity
Climbed up in a high church steeple
To be nearer God, so he might hand down
His word to all his people.

And in sermon script he daily wrote
What he thought was sent from heaven,
And he dropped it down on his people's heads
Two times one day in seven.

In his age God said, "Come down to die!"
And he in turn cried from the steeple,
"Where art thou, Lord?" and the Lord replied,
"Down here among my people!"

The priest who ministers on our behalf does not have such a condescending attitude toward His parishioners. Though He has "passed through the heavens" to minister before the "throne of grace" (cf. also Hebrews 8:1ff; 9:11ff), He does so as one who remembers what it is like to be down among the people. While on earth this priest sought no cloister, joined no monastic order. His parish was the street and the "masses" with which He was familiar were those of the human variety. We have a priest who intentionally "shared in [our] humanity" and was "made like his brothers in every way" (Hebrews 2:14, 17).

One important way that He was like His brothers was in His capacity to be tempted. Some Christians want no part of this kind of Christ. So intent are they to defend against the heresy that denies His divinity that they end up committing an equal heresy by denying His humanity. Equating temptation with sin, they resist any effort to portray Jesus as even being capable of experiencing temptation, much less yielding to it.

But while our author insists that Jesus was "without sin," he goes out of his way to point out that He was yet "tempted in every way, just as we are" (Hebrews 4:15; cf. 2:18). The tug of the forbidden, the lure of the prohibited, the appeal of self-gratification at the expense of integrity. He experienced them all. Because of who He was and what He had come to do, He was a special target of the tempter. This very fact accounts for the ultimate temptation Jesus faced—the one that our author really has in mind. It was the test of Gethsemane, when He sought to escape the ordeal of the crucifixion (Matthew 26:28ff). It was the temptation of Calvary when He heard the taunt to come down from the cross to prove that He was the Son of God (Matthew 27:40ff). It was the temptation to forsake His calling in view of the price He must pay to follow God (cf. also Mark 8:31-33). This, of course, is the very temptation that these Hebrew Christians are now facing.

Observing this, we can now understand what the author meant when he said that Jesus was able to "sympathize" with these beleaguered believers. Sympathy is most appreciated when it comes from someone who really understands what we are going through. What these Christians were going through was persecution because of their calling. If anyone could understand that, Jesus could. That is the reason our author chooses the term he does to describe Christ's ability to identify with their weaknesses. The Greek term that lies behind the word *sympathy* means literally "to suffer with." It describes the feelings of one who actually enters into the suffering of another. That is exactly what Jesus had done. Christ did not just feel *for* these Christians; He felt *with* them. As they have suffered because of their calling, so He has suffered because of His calling. For this reason He is uniquely qualified to "help those who are being tempted" (Hebrews 2:18).

Our Protocol Is Subject Unto God

> . . . and he was heard because of his reverent submission (Hebrews 5:7).

For a protocol to function effectively, he must have the full confidence of his superiors. There must be no question about the protocol's personal integrity or his unqualified loyalty to those who have authority over him. As we shall see, Jesus is uniquely qualified on both of these points to serve as our protocol of salvation before the ultimate Sovereign.

He Was Submissive in His Sinlessness (4:15)

Though Jesus shared in our temptations, He did not succumb to them. We who have succumbed find this difficult to comprehend. To be sure, Christ's sinlessness sets Him apart from us and puts us in awe of Him. But it also enables Him to minister on our behalf in a way that no priest "selected from among men" can.

Human priests and ministers are often little better than the blind leading the blind. Those of us who have accepted this calling are painfully aware of this fact. We can help men find the throne of grace only because we have been there ourselves so many times before. We sadly confess that our own sin is often as great as that of those whom we represent "in matters related to God." Our sin undermines our credibility and compromises our efforts to lead men before God's throne. We minister before God like lawyers pleading a case before a judge who has indicted us for the same crimes. Like the levitical priests of ancient Israel, we are constantly having to deal with our own sins before we can help other people deal with theirs (5:1-3;7:27). Our intercessory ministries are characterized by a tension between effort devoted to seeking forgiveness for others and effort devoted to seeking forgiveness for ourselves.

But the Protocol who pleads our case has no need to plead first His own. He owes no debt to God and bears no guilt before Him. He comes before God with impeccable credentials and complete credibility. Because He is "without sin," He already has the confidence of the Sovereign and is fully qualified to intercede before Him on our behalf. Beyond this, He also has our confidence. Unlike His human counterparts, our great high priest has been compromised by no scandal and discredited by no hypocrisy. He ministers with full integrity. Here at last is a spiritual leader whom we can trust, someone in whom we can believe, someone who lives by what He professes and who leads us along a path He has personally walked.

He Was Submissive in His Suffering (5:8, 9)

> Although he was a son, he learned obedience from what he suffered and, once made perfect, he became the source of eternal salvation for all who obey him . . . (Hebrews 5:8, 9).

The priest whom we follow received His theological education at a superior seminary. He mastered the most demanding curriculum, stood the most difficult of exams and still graduated at the top of His class. The lessons He needed to learn in order to be a priest could only be learned one way—the hard way. As our author puts it, He "learned obedience in the school of suffering" (New English Bible).

We, too, have attended this school. We, too, have learned from suffering, though in a radically different way from the way Jesus did. All too often, we suffer because we have sinned. We break God's laws, suffer the consequences, and then limp away smarting and hopefully smarter from our mistakes. By contrast, Jesus suffered because He refused to sin. The obedience He learned was by trial, not by trial and error. His suffering was not for sin but "for righteousness' sake." It taught Him the meaning of obedience by making Him pay the price for it. He "became obedient to death—even death on a cross" (Philippians 2:8)! Like none other, Jesus endured suffering to a degree that both tested and attested to the "perfection" of His devotion, proving it to be genuine and total.

"Because of his reverent submission," the "one who could save him from death" raised Him from the grave and made Him "the source of eternal salvation for all who obey him" (Hebrews 5:7-9). In other words, Christ's perfect obedience serves as both the means of our salvation (cf. Romans 5:19) and the model of how we can enjoy it. Completely sympathetic to human weakness and yet totally subject unto the divine will, our great high priest invites us to approach God's throne in search of "grace to help us in our time of need" (Hebrews 4:16). We can do so "with confidence" because our Protocol has paved the way for us. He knows exactly what we need and has the complete approval of the One who can supply it. As the rending of the temple curtain from top to bottom at the crucifixion dramatically symbolizes (Mark 15:38; Matthew 27:51; Hebrews 10:20), Christ has opened the door to the throne room of God. We can stand before God because Jesus stands with us.

CHAPTER SEVEN

Spiritual Never–never Land
Hebrews 5:11—6:3

Peter Pan is J. M. Barrie's classic tale of a boy who refuses to become a man. To escape the responsibilities of growing up, he runs away to Never-never Land to live among the fairies. Along with his companions, the Darling children, he experiences a series of great adventures that have been dramatized in British and American theater to the delight of millions. A statue of Peter Pan stands in a London square as a tribute to the charming antihero who personifies the spirit of perpetual childhood.

The Hebrew Christians would have liked Peter Pan. In a sense, his story is their story. Unwilling to accept the demands of spiritual adulthood, some of them are simply refusing to grow up into Jesus Christ. Aware of this, the author scolds the Hebrews for their infantile attitudes and urges them to move on to maturity. According to our text, the spiritual maturation of the Hebrew Christians will require a progression.

From Learning to Living

You are slow to learn . . . being still an infant . . . not acquainted with the teaching about righteousness (Hebrews 5:11, 13).

The Hebrew Christians are suffering from a learning disability. Their problem is not an intellectual one; it is spiritual. When the author chides them for being "slow to learn" (literally "dull of hearing"), he is not making fun of their lack of intelligence. He is scolding them for their conscious refusal to listen and learn. Their ignorance is willful. It is symptomatic of their arrested spiritual development. They have refused to "do their lessons" and, as a result, are still struggling with the "elementary truths" (or ABC's, Greek, *stoicheia*) when they should be moving on to the deeper things of God. They are still in grade school when, by this time, they "ought

55

to be teachers." They are still requiring "milk" when they ought to be on "solid food."

As a result, they are still "not acquainted with [or are unskilled in] the teaching about righteousness." This may refer to some incapacity for moral discrimination (Hebrews 5:14), or to some slowness to grasp the concept of righteousness that comes by faith rather than by good works (as in Pauline thought), or perhaps to some inability to teach properly about righteousness (cf. Hebrews 5:12). It may even refer to some lack of progress toward a correct understanding of the nature and work of Christ as taught by the Old Testament Scriptures, something to which our author is quite anxious to move on (cf. Hebrews 5:11; 7:1ff). Whatever shortcoming is being addressed here, it is obvious that the writer holds his readers personally responsible for it and characterizes it as a serious threat to their spiritual maturity.

In fact, spiritual ignorance, willful or otherwise, is always treated as a serious problem in Scripture. Refusing to subscribe to the irresponsible philosophy that "ignorance is bliss" or that "what you don't know can't hurt you," the Biblical authors universally condemn the ignorance of believer and unbeliever alike. Bemoaning the moral corruption of ancient Israel, the prophet Hosea warns that "a people without understanding will come to ruin" (Hosea 4:14). Jesus once condemned the Sadducees' rejection of the idea of resurrection as an error they perpetuated because they did "not know the Scriptures or the power of God" (Matthew 22:29). On numerous occasions, Paul prefaced his teachings to the churches by declaring that he did not want them to be ignorant (Romans 1:13; 11:25; 1 Corinthians 10:1; 12:1; 1 Thessalonians 4:13).

What we do not know *can* hurt us. The apostle Paul knew this from personal experience. He recalled his misguided past to young Timothy, remembering that he "was once a blasphemer and a persecutor" of the church, acting "in ignorance and unbelief" (1 Timothy 1:13). Paul's attacks on Christianity were the result of what he did not know. But the greatest crime of ignorance was not committed against man. No, it was committed against God. It happened on a lonely hill just outside the city of Jerusalem. There, ignorance accomplished what no other sin could do. It murdered the Son of God! From the rude timbers of the cross, the Lord of life looked down on His executors and said, "Father, forgive them for they know not what they do." Those words are more than an excuse. They are an accusation. They cry out with a deafening roar against the harm that ignorance can do. It was ignorance that killed Jesus—powerful, profane stupidity! On Calvary, ignorance raised a monument to itself. May it ever serve as a reminder of the harm that can come from what we do not know.

Harm has come to the Hebrews as a result of what they do not know. Like all students who shortcut the educational process, these students of Christ have ended up only cheating themselves. They are denying themselves the deeper truths of Christ toward which they should be stretching, and they are delaying the spiritual maturity toward which they should be pressing. While our author does not subscribe to the Aristotelian formula "to know the good is to do the good," he does suggest that to practice righteousness, one must at least understand what righteousness is. To such an understanding, he is now eager to lead his readers. As his words suggest, however, it will first require that they take their spiritual education seriously and come to appreciate the close connection between what they are to learn and how they are to live.

Mark Twain once quipped that he "never let his schooling get in the way of his education." It was his inimitable way of saying that not all of life's lessons are learned in the classroom. Take righteousness for example. Here is a subject that cannot be learned while sitting at a desk. Righteousness is something that must be learned by living in a right relationship with God. This is what our author means by characterizing the mature as those "who by constant use have trained themselves to distinguish good from evil" (Hebrews 5:14). These words refer to experience or skill acquired through habit or regular practice. The model our author uses is that of an athlete who systematically trains to compete. Righteousness—the kind that can discriminate between good and evil and follow the good—is not learned theoretically. It is learned experientially. It is learned in a classroom without walls, where faith encounters life and must pass the test of obedience. In this school our author now wishes to enroll the Hebrew Christians.

From Lingering to Leaving

Therefore let us leave the elementary teachings about Christ and go on to maturity (Hebrews 6:1).

As a college professor, I once helped a student register for a class only to learn that he had just completed the same course at another college. When I asked him why he was willing to invest time and money in a class he had already taken, he replied, "Because I know I can do well in it. I won't have to study in order to pass!" Five years later, this same student was still taking classes even though he had accumulated more than enough hours to graduate. Preferring the inherent comfort and security of his educational "nest" to the unpredictable and sometimes hostile "winds" of the real world, he was intentionally prolonging the preparation phase of his life at the expense of the performance phase.

To a degree, this seems to be the problem facing the Hebrew Christians. Intimidated by the challenges of living for Christ in a hostile world, they seem to be retreating into a shell of perpetual preparation. Instead of building upon the theological foundations of their faith, they are still laying those foundations over and over again. Instead of seeking new experiences in Christian living, they are content to repeat the old ones. Behaving like professional catechumens, they have become content to remain students of Christ instead of developing into servants of Christ.

One symptom of their refusal to mature has been their attempt to reduce Christianity into a select list of teachings and practices and make them normative for their experience of Christ. The author lists six different aspects of Christianity with which they have become preoccupied: "repentance from acts that lead to death, and of faith in God, instruction about baptisms, the laying on of hands, the resurrection of the dead, and eternal judgment" (Hebrews 6:1, 2). There is a great deal of scholarly speculation about the precise meaning and significance of this list, but there is general agreement that it constitutes a representative, but not exhaustive, list of the doctrines and practices of the apostolic church.

Of even greater significance for the meaning of the book of Hebrews, however, is the fact that it also constitutes a list of those teachings and practices that first-century Judaism and Christianity held in common. As such, it represents a list of Christian beliefs and practices that a first-century Jew could affirm without being distinctly Christian. For a group of Jewish converts who are on the verge of shrinking back from the high cost of discipleship, these aspects of their faith ironically supplied them with a vehicle for compromising their faith. By reducing Christianity to these particular teachings and practices, they could associate with Christianity without fully embracing it. Their religion is on the verge of becoming a grand pretension—having the appearance of Christianity but without its substance.

Many today seek to approach Christ on the same terms. They seek to reshape or redefine Christianity into a religion with which they can be comfortable yet to which they need not convert. As if seeking an inoculation against some dreaded disease, they want just enough of Christianity to keep from getting the real thing:

> I would like to buy $3 worth of God, please, not enough to explode my soul or disturb my sleep, but just enough to equal a cup of warm milk or a snooze in the sunshine. I don't want enough of Him to make me love a black man or pick beets with a migrant. I want ecstacy, not transformation; I want the warmth of the womb, not a new birth. I want a pound of the Eternal in a paper sack. I would like to buy $3 worth of God, please.[2]

You see, a religion is a very good place to hide from God. Affirming the doctrine of Christ is much easier than living in devotion to Christ. Performing Christian liturgy is much easier than practicing Christian piety. To the spiritually lazy, eschatology can mean escape from moral responsibility, the sacraments can serve as a substitute for true conversion, and doctrine can become a diversion from spiritual duty. Even Christianity, reduced only to a religion, is a very good place to hide from God!

Our author will not permit this of the Hebrew Christians. He will not let them substitute theological facts and religious forms for the substance of genuine faith. It's not that doctrine and ritual are unimportant. To the contrary, they are the "foundations" of their Christian experience. But they are not the totality of it. Foundations are meant to be built upon, not lived in. When Christianity is reduced to rehashing and rehearsing, it begins retreating. The key to Christian maturity is not the re-laying of the faith, but the releasing of the faith to grow to its full potential.

There's a bit of Peter Pan in all of us, this child in search of a Never-never Land. We seek some place where we never have to be responsible, never accountable, never anything but what we feel like being. It is a charming plot for a play, but it is a crippling plot for a life. Those who follow this script end up living beneath themselves. They build their nests on low branches and spend their lives majoring in the manageable. By deferring their maturity, they deny their

---

[2]Wilbur Rees, *$3.00 Worth of God* (Valley Forge, Judson Press, 1971).

potential and end up settling down into the fatal rut of mediocrity. As Shakespeare said,

> There is a tide in the affairs of men
> Which, taken at the flood, leads on to fortune;
> Omitted, all the voyage of their life
> Is bound in shallows and miseries.[3]

When the children of God refuse to become adults, the results are even more devastating. In the quest for spirituality, the failure to "go on" is a first step to "falling away." As the book of Hebrews goes on to suggest, arrested spiritual development may ultimately lead to apostasy (Hebrews 6:4-12). There is no "status quo" to righteousness. To stand still is to slip backwards. Perhaps Cromwell said it best when he wrote in his pocket Bible, *qui cessat esse melior cessat esse bonus,* "He who ceases to be better ceases to be good."[4]

God simply will not let us loiter our way through life. He will not let us idly slumber on some "bench" of blissful irresponsibility. The gospel awakens us from the stupor of our spiritual vagrancy and insists that we "move on"—on to maturation, on to graduation. Until, at last, we discover what all saints learn sometime before they die: the key to spirituality lies not in the achievement of it, but in the quest for it.

---

[3]William Shakespeare, *Julius Ceasar,* Act IV, Scene 3.

[4]William Barclay, *The Letter to the Hebrews* (Philadelphia: Westminster Press, 1955), p. 52.

CHAPTER EIGHT

Falling Out of Love With God

Hebrews 6:4-12

A man from a congregation where I once preached appeared late one night at my study door. I'm not quite sure what he sought from me. Perhaps it was just a sympathetic ear. It seems he had "fallen out of love" with his wife. He could not remember the day that it happened because it had not happened in a day. It had been a gradual thing, he said, like a dying coal or a slowly forming callous. The things that he had once given to her he had begun to give to others or no longer to give at all. And the things that he had once sought from her he had begun to seek from others or no longer to seek at all. "Love" had become "toleration," then "frustration," and then finally "nothing at all."

"It wasn't her fault," he admitted. "She was a good wife as wives go—loyal, supportive, dependable—a fine mother, too, to three wonderful daughters . . . they were all gone now, with lives of their own to live." He had just told her that he was leaving. He had tried to explain it to her, but she just couldn't understand. Instead, she had just stood there in stunned silence. He told her that he no longer loved her and that he could not go on faking it any more. And, besides that, he had found someone new now, and he had decided to move in with her. With that, he turned his back on her and twenty-five years of marriage and simply walked out of her life, never again to return.

I'll never forget that conversation. I am still haunted by its tragic story of love grown cold. But, as I read this text from the book of Hebrews, I tremble before an even greater tragedy—the tragedy of forsaken faith, of abandoned commitment, of broken promises, the tragedy of falling out of love with God. In this strongest warning of the book—and perhaps of all Scripture—the author confronts his readers with the grim possibility of their falling away from God into a spiritual state from which there is no return.

Severing Our Relationship With God

> It is impossible for those who have once been enlightened . . . if they
> fall away, to be brought back to repentance (Hebrews 6:4, 6).

Is it possible for a person once saved to fall away from God? The
book of Hebrews consistently answers in the affirmative (cf., for example, Hebrews 4:11; 10:26-39; 12:25). This text warns that the believer can actually fall into a spiritual state from which he cannot
return. "It is impossible for those who have once been enlightened . .
. if they fall away, to be brought back [literally, "renew again"] to repentance" (Hebrews 6:4-6). Many interpreters have stumbled over
that statement. Some have sidestepped it completely or attempted to
soften it in order to make it more compatible with the doctrine of the
eternal security of the saints. They argue that the word *impossible*
really means "difficult," or that those who "fall away" were really
not true believers in the first place. Then there are others who have
gone so far in the opposite direction as to say this passage teaches
that a single post-baptismal sin can permanently sever a believer's
relationship with God.

The proper understanding lies somewhere between these two ex-
treme positions. Important to note here is that the author's main subject is apostasy. He is not speaking of mere backsliding, of the
occasional shortcomings and failures that go with human weakness.
"Falling short" is not the same thing as "falling away." It is one
thing to yield to sin, contrary to the new life in Christ; but it is something very different to abandon that new life altogether. The
"falling" of which our author speaks is the equivalent of what he describes elsewhere when he speaks of one who "turns away from the
living God" (Hebrews 3:12).

Sometimes apostasy is a decisive step—a moment of truth in
which faith is consciously forsaken and commitment willfully abandoned. Such may have been the case for some of these wavering
saints as, in the face of persecution, they pondered the prospect of
renouncing Christ. More often, it is a slow and gradual process of
compromise and retrenchment. The conscience eventually becomes
so calloused that it can no longer be pricked. The heart grows so
cold that it can no longer love. The will becomes so stubborn it can
no longer believe. From such a state it is, at last, impossible to
renew people to repentance. It is impossible because they are no
longer capable of repenting. It is impossible because God at last has

"given them over" to their own choices (cf. Romans 1:18-32). His mercy has been mocked, His grace exploited, His Son disgraced for the last time.

But just who are the apostate, and how does one get himself into such a spiritual state that it is impossible to renew him to repentance? The author now moves in on this issue, painting two frightening portraits of forsaken faith and forfeited salvation. He contends that relationship with God can be irrevocably severed.

By Rejecting What God Has Done

> . . . who have tasted the heavenly gift, who . . . are crucifying the Son of God all over again and subjecting him to public disgrace (Hebrews 6:4, 6).

Apostasy is an ungrateful child. It takes stock of all that the Father has given and then turns its back and walks away. It says, "No, thank you," to salvation, "Some other time," to eternal life, and, "So what?" to the grace of God.

Roy Angel tells the story of a proud mother who attended her son's graduation from medical school. She had sacrificed much to get him through college. Unskilled and lacking in formal education, she was forced to perform the most menial and difficult labor in order to earn the thousands of dollars necessary to pay for her son's education. But now it all seemed worth it as he made his way forward to receive his degree. She stood at the back of the hall in a plain dress, her haggard face beaming with pride and joy. But the joy was soon shattered by a cruel ingratitude. Embarrassed by his mother's humble appearance and lack of cultural grace, the young man refused to acknowledge her, even to the point of turning his back whenever she approached in order to conceal the fact that he was her son.

In a senses the way some of the Hebrews were in danger of behaving toward Christ. Because of persecution, their relationship with Christ had become a liability to them, an embarrassment. Because of what their faith was costing them, they stood on the brink of apostasy, on the verge of forsaking their faith and "[turning] away from the living God" (Hebrews 3:12). In an effort to prevent this greatest of all tragedies, the author boldly confronts them with the implications of such a step.

He begins by rehearsing all that God has done for them. In sweeping phrases, he summarizes the blessings that have come from their relationship with Christ. They are those privileged ones "who have once been enlightened, who have tasted the heavenly gift, who have shared in the Holy Spirit, who have tasted the goodness of the word of God and the powers of the coming age" (Hebrews 6:4, 5). Some scholars see in these words specific references to their participation in the conversion process and the sacraments, while others see in them more general references to the characteristics and dynamics of the Christian experience. Whichever is the case, it is as clear from this text as any in the book that the people who are in danger of "falling away" are indeed Christians and full recipients of God's grace. As such, they have received the greatest gifts any person can receive. To reject them would be to reject the very things that God has given His only Son to provide.

But apostasy is more than ingratitude toward God's gifts. It is also blatant contempt for God's Son. To "fall away" in apostasy is to stand before the Christ of Calvary and, in full awareness of who He is and what He has done, to say, "This man deserves to die!" The author identifies apostasy with the greatest evil ever done. Forsaking Christ, he charges, is "crucifying the Son of God all over again" (Hebrews 6:6).

Crucify? Again? Surely not! We can conceive of those "who know not what they do" demanding Christ's death. But what about those who do know what they are doing—those who have acknowledged Jesus as God's Son and experienced His salvation? What kind of person could be party to the re-crucifying of Jesus? What kind of person could stand this side of Calvary and the empty tomb and still judge Him worthy of a disgraceful death? None of us? All of us? As Lois Cheney asks:

> Would we crucify Jesus today? It's not a rhetorical question for the mind to play with. I believe,
> We are each born with a body, a mind, a soul, and a handful of nails.[5]

How ugly is apostasy? How hideous is it to forsake Christ? It is as ugly as an unruly mob with an appetite for innocent blood. It is as hideous as an evil empire coldly plotting to silence the voice of truth. It is the ultimate blasphemy, the final profanity. It is to scorn

---

[5]Lois A. Cheney, *God is No Fool* (Nashville: Abingdon Press, 1969), p. 40.

the Savior and to mock God's grace. Modern apostates may call abandoning Christ "intellectual honesty" or "theological accommodation" or "situation ethics." The author of Hebrews calls it "crucifying the Son of God."

By Refusing What God Desires

> Land that produces thorns and thistles is worthless and is in danger of being cursed. In the end it will be burned (Hebrews 6:8).

Unfaithfulness is unfruitfulness. It is not just an inadvertent failure to bear fruit, but the conscious refusal to produce what God expects from our lives. The apostate is a well-watered, fertile field that yields only thorns and thistles. This motif of apostasy is a common one in Scripture. The prophet Isaiah depicts the nation Israel as a vineyard planted, cultivated, and nurtured by God but which, to His dismay, has yielded only bad fruit. Consequently, it is judged worthless and doomed to destruction (Isaiah 5:1-7). Jesus characterized His relationship with His followers as that of a vine to its branches, with the Father as the gardener who "cuts off every branch . . . that bears no fruit" (John 15:1ff).

The point of all these texts is that the Divine Gardener expects a harvest from His cultivation of our lives. Of the "soils" that receive the seed of His Word (see the parable of the sower/soils in Matthew 13:3ff), only those that let it take root and grow and produce a crop will experience the ultimate blessings of faith. Unproductive fields forfeit faith's reward.

Erskine Caldwell's book, God's Little Acre, is a modern parable of how a life that refuses to produce what God desires eventually comes under a "curse." Its main character, Ty-Ty Walden, inherits a beautiful farm. When Ty-Ty marries, his wife's pastor agrees to perform the ceremony provided Ty-Ty will give God one-tenth of his land under cultivation. Ty-Ty consents, marking God's acre with a large, eight-foot iron cross.

In time, however, Ty-Ty comes to believe that gold lies just beneath the surface of his land. Instead of farming the land, he decides to dig for his hidden treasure. Frustrated by his fruitless search, he finally concludes that the gold must lay under God's little acre. In a moment of truth, he decides to move the cross from one acre to another and to dig in its place. Once he starts this, he cannot seem to stop. For fifteen years, he digs "his" land, moves the cross, and digs some more, until he turns the farm into a wasteland. In the end, his family leaves him and the bank takes possession of his land. His life is in ruins because he has failed to appreciate what had been entrusted to him, and he has refused to honor the God who had provided it.

This story is a portrait of apostasy akin to that which the author of Hebrews sets before us. Rejecting all that God has done, the one who "falls away" consciously refuses to acknowledge the claim of the cross upon his life. He pulls up the marker of "God's acre" and makes the field his own. There begins a process that, if given a chance, will lead one down a path from which there is no return, a path into a sin of which he will not or cannot repent. The fertile land becomes "worthless and is in danger of being cursed," but the farmer no longer cares because he is no longer a farmer. He is something else—something his friends, his family, and even his God no longer recognize.

Sustaining Our Relationship With God

> Even though we speak like this, dear friends, we are confident of better things in your case—things that accompany salvation (Hebrews 6:9).

Though the author of Hebrews warns these wavering Christians of the very real danger of reaching a spiritual point (or a process) of no return, he is quick to affirm his confidence that these believers have not yet approached it. In the manner of the ancient Hebrew prophets, the author now balances the stick of warning with the carrot of encouragement. With genuine affection, he urges his "dear friends" to take whatever steps necessary to preserve their redemptive relationship with Christ. He urges them to manifest those attitudes and actions that "will make their hope sure" and allow them to "inherit what has been promised."

By Relying on the Discernment of God

> God is not unjust; he will not forget your work and the love you have shown him as you have helped his people and continue to help them (Hebrews 6:10).

For most of us, justice is an unpleasant subject. It is something that happens when our dog gets in the neighbor's garbage, when we "underestimate" our taxes, or when we "forget" our fishing license. It is a blue light flashing in our rear-view mirror, a certified letter that comes in the mail, or a nervous confrontation with an unsmiling face. It always seems to catch us at our worst.

And then there is the justice of God. Now there is something to fear. We have read of the flood, of Sodom and Gomorrah, and of the wilderness strewn with the bodies of the rebellious. We understand what a "terrifying thing [it is] to fall into the hands of the living God" (Hebrews 10:31, New American Standard Bible). And since we have all been on His wrong side before, most of us would just as soon stay out of His court. Chafing beneath the "yoke" of the divine justice, we end up spending much of our lives trying to wiggle out from beneath it. We go about looking for loopholes, trying to beat the system, trying to cheat the executioner. All the while, we have this fearful dread of an inescapable day in court. Our hearts warm to the idea of God's mercy, but, at the thought of His justice, our palms start to sweat.

A deeper look at God's justice, however, reveals its other face. God's justice is a two-edged sword, a scale with two sides. It does more than mete out judgment and punishment. It also weighs out vindication and reward. God's scrutiny of man notices more than the evil of which he is guilty. It also takes note of the good of which he is capable. "God is not unjust," insists our author. "He will not forget your work and the love you have shown him" (Hebrews 6:10). The justice of God is about more than condemnation. It is about affirmation. The same God who threatens evil with punishment also promises reward for good.

The good that we do will not go unnoticed by God. Confidence in that fact helps to shape the Christian's perspective of life and to sustain faithful service. Witness, for example, the testimony of Dr. James W. Bashford, the noted scholar and university president. At the very height of his academic profession, he left his position to become a missionary to China. Some time later, a former colleague visited him on the field in China. Witnessing Bashford's humble mission in a remote village, his friend asked, "Why do you bury yourself away in China?"

"Because," he replied, "I believe in resurrection."

The good that we do is not "buried"—not forever. Though unnoticed or unappreciated in this world, it will be honored in the next. Though crushed by the evil one and assigned to the grave of obscurity, by the power of the Just One it will rumble in the ground and rise to its reward. As the empty tomb vindicates the Christ of the cross, so also does it vindicate those who do good in His name. We can rely on that, we can rest in it. Faith in God's fairness can sustain our relationship with Him.

By Remaining Devoted to God

> . . . the love you have shown him as you have helped his people and continue to help them. We want each of you to show this same diligence to the very end (Hebrews 6:10, 11).

Love is the cement of all human relationships. It has the power to overcome all of the things that threaten their viability. Love bears the unbearable and forgives the unforgivable. It heals relationships when they begin to tear apart, and it rekindles them when they start to grow cold and die. It sustains them when all else fails. People may come together for many reasons, but they will stay together because of love.

This is also true of our relationship with God. People come to God for a variety of reasons. Some seek Him out of fear of the consequences for failing to do so. Others come to Him out of a desire for some reward. But those who stay with God, who abide in Him and remain faithful to Him, do so out of love. As Augustine once said of the prodigal, "A darkened heart in the distant country. For it is not by our feet but by our affections that we either leave or return to God."

Loving God is the title of Charles Colson's autobiography. That ought to be easy enough. After all, He is the one who made the world and all who are in it. He is the author and sustainer of life, the giver of every good and perfect gift. He is the God who forgives us of our sins and receives us unto himself. He is the God who so loved the world that He gave his only begotten Son. Who could possibly be easier to love?

But deep in the recesses of our hearts lie other feelings toward God—feelings that have grown out of living in His world and the difficulty of trying to reconcile what He allows to happen with who He proclaims himself to be. We have heard He is a just God, yet we observe that He permits injustice to overtake the just and tragedy to befall the most undeserving. We believe Him to be a God who answers prayer, yet, when we pray, we do not always get what we ask for. We know that He is a God who loves His children, but we observe that they continue to suffer and die. If we let them, the absurdities and inequities of life can begin to chip away at our affections for its Giver and Sustainer.

The persecution that the Hebrews are experiencing is evidently mounting just such a challenge to the love they have for God. It is a true love, deep and genuine, expressing itself in the way God most desires it—in concern for their fellowman. It is affection in action, manifesting itself in kindnesses shown to their suffering brothers and sisters. The loving deeds of "those earlier days" are detailed in Hebrews 10:32-34. But time has begun to test their devotion. The persecution wears on with no end in sight, and they are now faced with the prospect of living and dying with a love for God that has no visible reward. Accordingly, they are now prepared to discover what loving God is all about.

What does it mean to love God? It is to bind oneself to God with uncompromising devotion and unconditional affection. To love God is to take Him on His own terms and to submit to Him with the unqualified conviction that, in spite of life's inequities, He really is who He claims to be. It is to love God without proof of His existence, with only promise of His reward. If necessary, it is to sit with Job on the ash heap of life with all that we hold dear crumbling around us and yet to profess, "The Lord gave and the Lord has taken away; may the name of the Lord be praised" (Job 1:21). It is to say with the poet:

My God, I love Thee;
Not because I hope for heaven thereby,
Nor yet because who love Thee not
Must die eternally.

Thou, O my Jesus,
Thou didst me upon the cross embrace;
For me didst bear the nails, the nails and spear,
And manifold disgrace.

Why, then why, O blessed Jesus Christ,
Should I not love Thee well?
Not for the hope of winning heav'n,
Or of escaping hell;

Not with the hope of gaining aught,
Not seeking a reward;
But as Thyself hast loved me,
O ever loving Lord!

E'en so I love Thee, and will love,
And in Thy praise will sing;
Solely because Thou art my God,
And my Eternal King.[6]

Such love is the antidote to apostasy. It empowers faithfulness when all else fails.

The believer who falls away from God does so because he has first fallen out of love with Him. The apostate is the believer who coldly, willfully, and deliberately says to God, "I no longer love You, and I choose to live my life without You." As with the demise of a human relationship, apostasy is a very sad and tragic business. It is a slippery slide into the total absence of affection for God. And in case you have any question about what lies at its end, give heed to the haunting confession of Jean-Paul Sartre following his descent into atheism:

> My retrospective illusions are in pieces. Martyrdom, salvation, immortality: all are crumbling; the building is falling in ruins. I have caught the Holy Ghost in the cellars and flung him out of them. Atheism is a cruel, long-term business. I have gone through it to the end. I see clearly, I am free from illusions, I know my real tasks, and I must surely deserve a civic prize; for about ten years I have been a man who is waking up, cured of a long, bittersweet madness, who cannot get away from it, who cannot recall his old ways without laughing and who no longer has any idea what to do with his life. I have become once again the traveller without a ticket that I was at seven: the ticket-collector has entered my compartment and is looking at me, but less sternly than he once did: in fact, all he wants is to go away and let me complete the journey in peace; as long as I give him a valid excuse of some kind, he will be satisfied. Unfortunately I cannot find one and, besides, do not even want to look for one: we shall go on talking together, ill at ease, as far as Dijon where I know quite well that no one is waiting for me.[7]

---

[6]Anonymous, seventeenth-century Latin poem, tr. by Edward Caswall (New York: Carl Fischer, Inc., 1954).

[7]Jean-Paul Sartre, *Les Mots* (Paris, 1964); Eng. tr.: *Words* (London: Hamish Hamilton, 1964), pp. 171-172.

I do not pretend to know all that brings a man to such a state, but of this I am quite sure; I do not wish to join him.

PRAYER:
O make me thine forever;
And should I fainting be,
Lord let me never, never
Outlive my love to thee.[8]

---

[8]Isaac Watts, *The Methodist Hymnal,* 1966.

CHAPTER NINE

So Help Me, Me

Hebrews 6:13-20

In *Uncle Tom's Cabin,* there is a scene where a Biblical promise is read to a slave laboring in the smothering heat of a cotton field:

> "Come unto me all ye who labor and I will give you rest."
> "Dem's good words," the slave replies. "But who sez um?"
> "You see it makes all the difference in the world who sez um."

A promise is only as good as the person who makes it. For this reason, we have learned to take most of them with a grain of salt. Life has taught us that "promises are made to be broken." We have been both victim and victimizer in the underhanded business of the unkept word.

This is at least one reason we are so skeptical of the promises of God. After all, we have broken so many of our promises to Him, how could we ever expect Him to keep the ones He has made to us? What's more, some of the long-term promises of God seem to be invalidated by our short-term life experiences. Seeing what happens to Christians in this world we, like the Hebrews, have a tendency to be a bit incredulous toward our prospects for enjoying what is promised us in the world to come.

Addressing the growing doubts of these suffering saints toward the promises of God, the author now seeks to reassure his readers that, though their immediate circumstances can be threatened by the evil that is in this world, their ultimate destiny cannot. It is fixed. It is settled. It is guaranteed by the One who always keeps His word.

God's Immutable Purpose

> God wanted to make the unchanging nature of his purpose very clear to the heirs of what was promised (Hebrews 6:17).

The Christian faith asks us to stake our destinies upon the promises of God. For this reason, it is very important that we understand the nature of those promises and know how they are realized in our lives.

God's Promises Are Credible

God's promises are grounded in His character. He has the absolute ability and the uncompromising integrity to fulfill them. They are, therefore, completely credible. The spiritual giant David Livingston understood this. His favorite Biblical verse was one of the great promises of Scripture, "Lo, I am with you alway, even to the end of the world" (Matthew 28:20, King James Version). His biographers tell us that, whenever he was confronted with some special danger or difficulty, he would write the text afresh in his journal along with this affirmation: "It is the word of a Gentleman of the strictest and most sacred honour, and that's an end of it."[9]

"The word of a Gentleman"—such are the promises of God. They are reliable, guaranteed by someone "of the strictest and most sacred honour." So sacred is His honor that a broken promise would compromise His very being, undermine His very Godness. For this reason, it is "impossible" for Him to lie.

So important is it to God that His children believe in His promises that He has on several occasions confirmed them by a sacred oath. Condescending to the human need for reassurance, He has voluntarily raised His right hand to swear before man by the highest power in the universe, the only authority by which He is bound—himself. "By myself I have sworn, my mouth has uttered in all integrity a word that will not be revoked" (Isaiah 45:23; cf. also Isaiah 62:8; Jeremiah 22:5; 44:26; 49:13; 51:14; Amos 6:8; especially Genesis 22:16). It is as if God is saying, "I will uphold My promises and keep My word, so help Me, Me!"

God's promises reflect His intention to accomplish His will in His world. With respect to both His sovereignty and His holiness, God's promise and God's oath are "two unchangeable things" (Hebrews 6:18). They are fixed and immutable. They are as certain as the rising and the setting of the sun (cf. Jeremiah 33:20, 21). We can ground our hope for our eternal destinies on the credibility of God's word of promise.

---

[9]John Phillips, *Exploring Hebrews* (Chicago: Moody Press, 1981), p. 96

God's Promises Are Conditional

But, as the author of Hebrews has repeatedly warned, not all of God's children "inherit what has been promised" (Hebrews 6:12; cf. Hebrews 3:16—4:11). This is not due to any failing on the part of God. It is due to some failing on the part of man. For attached to God's promises to man are His expectations of man. And, while the eternal promises of God are not dependent upon the actions of men, it is the consistent testimony of Scripture that an individual's enjoyment of those promises is contingent upon his fulfillment of certain conditions (cf. especially Psalm 89:28-37). This was true of God's promise to David, "**If** your sons are careful of their way, to walk before Me in truth . . . you shall not lack a man on the throne of Israel (1 Kings 2:4, New American Standard Bible; cf. also 1 Kings 9:4-7; Psalm 132:11-12). It was true of God's promises to Israel through Moses. The Scriptures make it clear that Israel's peace, prosperity, and security in the promised land were directly tied to their obedience to the law of Moses (cf. Leviticus 26; Deuteronomy 4:23ff). If they disobeyed that law, God promised them curses instead of blessings.

This element of conditionality is also present in the text that our author specifically chooses to cite in illustration of the reliability of God's promises. It was upon the occasion of the near sacrifice of Isaac that God "swore by himself" to Abraham, ". . . **because** you have done this and have not withheld your son, your only son, I will surely bless you . . . **because** you have obeyed me" (Genesis 22:16-18; cf. also 17:1, 2; 18:19). Abraham "received what was promised" because he met God's condition. The condition upon which our author here focuses is that of "patience" (Greek, *makrothumasas*, Hebrews 6:15, cf. also verse 12). It is but another term in his vocabulary of "faithfulness." It refers to the patience required to wait for God to keep His promises, and carries with it the idea of "endurance" or "forbearance."

Patience is part of the price of inheriting God's promises. As virtues go, it is one that modern man has lost. In this up-to-the-minute world, there are very few things for which we are willing to wait. One might characterize the "now generation" as that which "hatches eggs with a blow torch." It seems we cannot wait for things to take their natural course. Perhaps the fitting symbol for our time is the Polaroid camera. Push the button, out comes the picture—so typical of our passion for having things "right now." Somewhere in our headlong rush into the future, we have forgotten how to wait.

Some of the Hebrews have forgotten how to wait, too. A mood of impatience has begun to settle over these tired saints as persecution continues to take its toll. God had made certain promises about the future and, as yet, nothing has happened. "Salvation?" "Rest?" "Reward?" Where are they? The challenge of the "scoffers" that Peter said would arise has, perhaps, begun to seep in through the cracks of their fractured faith. "Where is this 'coming' he promised? Ever since our fathers died, everything goes on as it has since the beginning of creation" (2 Peter 3:4). For some Christians, delay in the fulfillment of God's promises leads to doubt over the fulfillment of God's promises. They interpret His "slowness" to act as His inability or unwillingness to act. Like the two nondescript hobos in Samuel Beckett's fantasy, *Waiting for Godot* (God), they eventually tire of waiting for this mysterious Person who promised to meet them but delays His arrival.

Actually, God has a habit of making man wait. The parables of Jesus abound with this theme. There is the farmer or the husbandman or the master who travels to a far country, leaving his goods in the hands of his servants, and who, as often as not, delays his return. He waits intentionally—as if to watch and see what his servants will do with the resources he has left behind. In a similar way, God made Abraham wait. The one whom God called to be the "father of a great multitude" had to wait eighty-six years to become a father at all (of Ishmael, Genesis 16:15) and even then, it was not the child that God had in mind. It was not until he reached the ripe old age of one hundred, some twenty-five years after God had called him (Genesis 21:5; cf. 12:4), that he saw the first generation of the "great nation" that would come from him. We learn later that it was all a part of a "test" of faith that would culminate in the command to sacrifice Isaac at Moriah (Genesis 22:1ff). Through his "faith and patience," Abraham learned that his destiny lay not in the thing that was promised but in the God who made the promise, the "Lord who provides" (Genesis 22:14). "After waiting patiently, Abraham received what was promised" (Hebrews 6:15). That is what these Hebrews must now do, and it is what we must do. Those whom God calls are called to wait.

Man's Immovable Prospect

God did this so that . . . we who have fled to take hold of the hope offered to us may be greatly encouraged. We have this hope as an anchor for the soul, firm and secure (Hebrews 6:18, 19).

Some years ago, one of our nation's submarines sank off the coast of Massachusetts, becoming a prison for its crew. Ships were rushed to the scene and divers were sent down to see whether anything could be done to save them. The men in the submarine clung desperately to life as their oxygen supply was slowly being exhausted. Communication with the divers was maintained by tapping out Morse code on the steel hull that surrounded them. Time was running out. After a seemingly endless pause, a question was slowly and weakly tapped out from inside the submarine: "Is . . . there . . . any . . . hope?" With their last breath they were still clinging to the last thing men let go of—hope.

"Is there any hope?" It seems our world has always been asking that question. People were asking it when Christianity was born. To a world that Paul described as "without hope and without God" (Ephesians 2:12) came the church with this bold affirmation: "Praise be to the God and Father of our Lord Jesus Christ! In his great mercy he has given us new birth into a living hope through the resurrection of Jesus Christ from the dead" (1 Peter 1:3). There is nothing more "Christian" than hope. Along with faith and love, it is one of the three principle graces of the Christian life (cf. 1 Corinthians 13:13). The Bible is the most hope-filled book in the world. It says we are a people who are "saved by hope" (Romans 8:24), who should "not . . . grieve like the rest of men, who have no hope" (1 Thessalonians 4:13), and who live "resting on the hope of eternal life, which God . . . promised before the beginning of time" (Titus 1:2). Our God is a "God of hope" (Romans 15:13) and everything written in Scripture was "written to teach us, so that through endurance and the encouragement of the Scriptures we might have hope" (Romans 15:4).

The author now encourages the Hebrews to "take hold" of this hope as the great prospect, the great expectation, of the Christian life. In so doing, he identifies the basis of Christian hope and the blessings that it holds for these beleaguered saints.

The Character of Christian Hope

In the musical *South Pacific*, Mary Martin sang, "I'm stuck like a dope with a thing called hope." While that is lovely sentiment, it is not at all what the author of Hebrews means by *hope*. Those cheerful expressions—"all will be well," "look on the bright side," "hope for the best"—that we are prone to use are mostly just sentiment. Divorced from reality or any sense of destiny, they are nothing more than empty optimism, wishful thinking—vain attempts to sustain us in the face of unbearable disasters and unrealized dreams.

The paths of life are strewn with the victims of misplaced hope—people who have been burned by a relationship, betrayed by a friend, disillusioned by a cause gone sour, disappointed by a personal failure. With great expectations, we set out to seize life only to discover that it has a better hold on us than we do on it and that many of our dreams are beyond our ability to turn into reality. Unfulfilled hope "makes the heart sick," said the writer of Proverbs (13:12). How well he speaks to our age. For too many years, we have been putting our hopes in the wrong things and have come away sick at heart.

There is, at last, only one cure for such a sickness. It is to ground our hopes in that which does not fail. The key to a lasting hope that does not disappoint rests not in *for what* we hope, but *in whom* we hope. Christian hope is not based on the dreams and schemes of men but upon the nature and character of God. It is as firm as God's promises, as dependable as His determination to accomplish His will. It is not a hope in the future alone, but in the God who holds the future. It is, as Paul reminds us, "*Christ* in you, the hope of glory" (Colossians 1:27). As long as our hope is founded in Him, it will never fail us; it will never let us down.

The Consequences of Christian Hope

This sure and steadfast hope secures many blessings for the Christian. They are enjoyed in this life and in the life to come. Appealing to that in which his readers might find refuge, our author focuses upon two of hope's consequences that were especially meaningful for the Hebrews. They also hold great meaning for Christians today.

Hope is the Christian's asylum. In ancient Israel, special places were set aside where persons accused of serious crimes might find temporary asylum while their case was being heard. Those accused of manslaughter could flee to one of six "cities of refuge" where they were safe from their accusers until their trial was over (cf. Numbers 35:10ff; Deuteronomy 4:41-43; 19:2ff; Joshua 20). Others sought asylum at God's sanctuary by fleeing to the altar and taking hold of its horns (or corners; cf. 1 Kings 1:50, 51; 2:28). Our author seems to have this idea in mind when he describes himself and his fellow believers as "we who have fled to take hold of the hope offered to us" (Hebrews 6:18). He is saying that, for the Christian, hope functions as a temporary asylum until the time of our final vindication. Like a person wrongly accused, we flee by faith to God's altar, where we find refuge while Jesus pleads our case and secures our redemption. Even though we may not see our vindication in this life, we live in hope of it because, through His resurrection and ascension, the one "who went before us" has been vindicated and intercedes before God "on our behalf."

Hope is also the Christian's anchor. It functions as a spiritual mooring to bind us by strong cords to the "Rock of our salvation" (Psalm 95:1). This metaphor of hope as an anchor is found only here in the New Testament but was especially meaningful to early Christians, as is witnessed by the widespread presence of the anchor on their jewelry, coins, and gravestones. Hope, like an anchor, gives security and stability to our lives (souls). It is cast upward, where it lays hold of Christ and the promises God offers us through Him. As Priscilla J. Owens has expressed it in one of our hymns:

> We have an anchor that keeps the soul
> Steadfast and sure while the billows roll,
> Fastened to the Rock which cannot move,
> Grounded firm and deep in the Savior's love.

Another Christian song writer, Frances Havergal, lived a life anchored by such hope. On the last day of her life, she asked a friend to read to her from Isaiah, chapter 42. When her friend got to verse 6, she heard these words for the last time, "I, the Lord, have called you in righteousness, and will hold your hand; I will keep you. . . ." With a voice weakened by the ravages of disease, Frances Havergal whispered, "Called, held, kept—I can go home on that."[10]

And so can we. As the writer of Proverbs reassures us, it is not only in life that the we can hope but, "the righteous hath hope in his death" (Proverbs 14:32, KJV). In the final analysis, this is hope's highest blessing, its finest hour.

Witness the passing of scientist Michael Faraday. As this great Christian lay dying, one of his colleagues came to his bedside. In typical scholarly fashion, he asked, "Well, Michael, what are your speculations?" Faraday's reply was given with serene confidence:

---

[10]John C. Maxwell, *Deuteronomy* (Waco: Word [Communicator's Commentary series], 1989), p. 349.

"Speculations? I have none. I know whom I have believed. I rest my soul on certainties."

So it is with the child of God. While the moment of our death may be shrouded in mystery, its final outcome is not. Our fate is fixed, our destiny is determined. It is guaranteed by the promises of God and secured by the resurrection of His only Son. "Let us hold unswervingly to the hope we profess, for he who promised is faithful" (Hebrews 10:23).

CHAPTER TEN

The Perfect Priest

Hebrews 7:1-28

Among the various rites of spring, like courting and baseball, is one that is peculiar to the church. It is a "rite of passage," so to speak. As the temperature starts to rise and church attendance starts to fall, visions of "greener pastures" begin to dance in the minds of frustrated pastors. Before you can say "official notice," the "Spirit" leads the pastor on to another ministry, leaving his "faithful flock" with the difficult task of finding a replacement. In ecclesiastical terms, it is known as "calling a new minister," and it can prove to be a high drama of intrigue, misrepresentation, bribery, and occasionally even providence.

Now, if the the truth be known, most church members have very definite ideas about what they want and do not want in a minister. If allowed, this "wish list" can translate into a job description before which even the most gifted would tremble. Someone has compiled a list of those qualifications requested most often by churches:

He is twenty-six years old and has been preaching for thirty years.

He is tall and short, thin and heavy set, and handsome.

He has one brown eye and one blue. He parts his hair in the middle with the left side dark and straight and the right side light and curly.

He preaches exactly twenty minutes and then sits down.

He condemns sin but never hurts anyone's feelings.

He works from 8:00 AM to 10:00 PM in every type of work from preaching to custodial service.

He makes $100 a week, wears good clothes, buys good books, has a nice family, drives a good car, and gives $50 a week to the church.

He has a burning desire to work with teenagers and spends all of his time with the older folks.

He makes fifteen calls a day on church members, spends all his time evangelizing the unchurched, and is never out of the office.

The Jews of the first century also had certain expectations of their minister, the high priest. Their concept of the perfect priest, however, derived not from their own personal wish list but from a job description written by God himself. These same standards are now used by our author as a means of presenting Jesus as the great high priest of these Jewish converts, far superior to any priest who had served them in their former religion. In so doing, he makes his unique contribution to the rich and varied New Testament portraits of Jesus Christ.

As to why the author chose to devote so much attention to the priesthood of Christ, we may suggest two potential answers, both growing out of the particular circumstances of his readers. First of all, these converts had come out of Judaism to become Christians, and they were now in danger of going back into it. Of the many attractive features of their former religion, the authority figure of the high priest and the tangible evidence of God's presence and forgiveness that his ministry seemed to provide must have had a special appeal to a people called to live in faith of what they "do not see" (Hebrews 11:1). Second, the messianic hope of late, pre-Christian Judaism had come to expect an "anointed one" who would function as a priest. Thus, by focusing on the "high priesthood" of Jesus, the author presents him to his readers both as Messiah and as the only one truly capable of obtaining their redemption and helping them draw near to God.

To present Jesus as a great high priest to someone well-versed in Judaism was no small task. The law of Moses was quite specific as to who could be a priest and, at first sight, Jesus of Nazareth did not seem to meet the qualifications. This leads our author into an involved exegesis of several Old Testament texts to prove that Jesus was indeed a high priest, superior in every way from the ones who had descended from Aaron.

The Superior Line of Our Great High Priest

> . . . one in the order of Melchizedek, not in the order of Aaron (Hebrews 7:11).

In ancient Israel, priests were not "called" to their profession. They were "born" to it. Unlike Israel's prophets, the priests had to descend from a particular line. According to the law of Moses, the high priest must be from the tribe of Levi and be a direct descendant of Aaron. Now this fact posed a problem for the priesthood of

Christ, for, as the author readily acknowledges, "our Lord descended from Judah, and in regard to that tribe Moses said nothing about priests" (Hebrews 7:14).

This problem is solved by demonstrating that Jesus is a priest from another order, a priestly line that existed prior to the order of Aaron and was superior to it—the order of Melchizedek. Arguing by analogy and by typology (a comparison made on the basis of a person, place, or event that anticipates and foreshadows a superior person, place, or event that comes later), the author is able to show his readers how the ancient priesthood of Melchizedek typifies the priesthood of Christ.

Few characters in the Old Testament are more mysterious or more intriguing than Melchizedek (cf. Genesis 14:17-20; Psalm 110:4). The Jews of the first century had a special interest in him, a fact that may have contributed to the amount of attention given him by our author. A king of "Salem" (literally, of "peace," perhaps the city of Jerusalem) and "priest of God Most High," he appears suddenly on the stage of Biblical history without any reference to his ancestors, birth, or death. This, argues our author, anticipates the greater and truly eternal life and line of Jesus (Hebrews 7:3, 16, 17, 23, 24). The fact that he both blessed Abraham and received the tithe from him is cited by our author as further proof that Melchizedek was superior to Abraham and, therefore, to Abraham's descendant, Aaron (Hebrews 7:1-10). Thus, on the basis of its precedence and nature, the priestly line of Melchizedek is greater than that of Aaron. Since Jesus is of Melchizedek's order, His priesthood is superior to that of Aaron's descendants, who minister on behalf of the Jews.

The Superior License of Our Great High Priest

> The former regulation is set aside and because it was weak and useless
> . . . and a better hope is introduced, by which we draw near to God
> (Hebrews 7:18, 19).

In most communities today, ministers must be properly licensed in order to function as religious practitioners. They are required to show proof of ordination and to demonstrate their intent to minister in good faith under the auspices of a recognized church or religious authority. In a way, this was also true of the priests of Israel. They, too, underwent ordination and had their ministries approved by a recognized religious authority. The authority by which they ministered, however, was nothing less than the law of Moses.

Now, as religious authorities go, the law of Moses was a sound one, sanctioned by God himself. It was undermined, however, by one fatal flaw. Its power to secure man's relationship with God was limited by man's ability to obey it. To those who kept it, the law was an instrument of life (Romans 10:5), but, to those who broke it, the law was an instrument of death (Romans 7:10-13). Since all of God's children have broken His law, we are all under its condemnation. Even the priests, appointed by this law to seek forgiveness for God's disobedient children by offering sacrifices on their behalf, did not live up to their calling but were themselves "weak" and needed to offer sacrifices for their own sins (Hebrews 7:27, 28). Thus, the whole system of salvation broke down around human inability to keep it.

This, it seems, had been anticipated by God all along and had been part of His plan to prepare us for the coming of Jesus Christ. Centuries before the birth of Christ, God had promised through the prophet Jeremiah that he would "make a new covenant [contract between man and God] with the house of Israel and with the house of Judah" (Hebrews 8:8-12; cf. Jeremiah 31:31-34). This covenant, our author tells us, is the very one now being "mediated" by Jesus Christ, having taken effect upon His sacrificial death (Hebrews 8:7; 9:15-20). The New Covenant, which is fully able to secure our salvation, has made the Old Covenant (the law of Moses) "obsolete" (Hebrews 8:13). Having taught us that we cannot save ourselves, the law has served its purpose and can now be "set aside" (Hebrews 10:9; cf. Galatians 3:10-25). In Christ, we are called to embrace the "new order" (Hebrews 9:10), the "new and living way" (Hebrews 10:20) that God has raised up in its place.

In Christ, God offers us a new way to be saved—a way that is not dependent upon human ability to keep commandments but upon God's determination to keep His promises. In Christ, God will do for us what we could not do for ourselves. "I will put my laws in their minds and write them on their hearts" (Hebrews 8:10; cf. Jeremiah 31:33). Instead of trying to live up to His words, we will live by them. "I will forgive their wickedness and will remember their sins no more" (Hebrews 8:12; cf. Jeremiah 31:34). Instead of trying to gain our forgiveness, we will be granted it. "I will be their God, and they will be my people" (Hebrews 8:10; cf. Jeremiah 31:33). Instead of His subjects or His students, we are invited to become His sons.

At the center of this system is a Savior, a great high priest through whose ministry we can at last "draw near to God" (Hebrews 7:19).

Here is one who is able to do what no human priest could ever do—to secure our complete and eternal salvation (Hebrews 7:25). Here, at last, is a minister whose coattails we can ride to Heaven. He ministers not by the authority of some denominational headquarters or some local congregation. This priest has been licensed by God himself, ordained by His very oath (Hebrews 7:20-22), to minister on our behalf.

The Superior Life of Our Great High Priest

> One who has become a priest not on the basis of a regulation as to his ancestry but on the basis of the power of an indestructible life (Hebrews 7:16).

Bishop Quayle once remarked that "the art of preaching is not the art of preparing and delivering a sermon. It is the art of preparing and delivering a preacher." In that remark, he affirmed something veteran Christians have always known. The key to successful ministry does not lie in the minister's charisma or his craft. It rests in his character. On balance, a minister can lead his people along the path to spiritual maturity only as far as he himself has gone. While, in some professions, life and work are not necessarily interdependent, they are absolutely inseparable in the ministry. Ministry is not just something one does. It is something one is.

It is in this dimension of Christ's priesthood that He displays the greatest superiority over the priests of Aaron's line. To demonstrate that superiority, the author of Hebrews focuses on two aspects of Christ's life to which the Aaronic priests simply could not measure up: His moral excellence and His immortality.

Call it "job description" or "occupational hazard," personal holiness has always been expected by God of those who minister before Him. It is an expectation that His ministers have always had difficulty living up to. Nadab and Abihu, probably under the influence of alcohol (cf. Leviticus 10:8-11), offered "unauthorized fire before the Lord, contrary to his command" (Leviticus 10:1). For this profanity they lost their lives, while their father, Aaron looked on in stunned silence (Leviticus 10:1-3). Centuries later, the priest Eli looked on in horror while his sons, Hophni and Phineas, abused their priestly office for dishonest gain and sexual immorality (1 Samuel 2:12-17, 22-25). Eli's failure to restrain them eventually led to the priestly lines being passed on through another family (1 Samuel 2:27-36; 3:13, 14). The priest Abiathar got himself involved in a political plot that backfired and caused him to lose his office (1 Kings 1:7-10; 2:26, 27). Hosea accused the priests of his day of "feeding on the sins of God's people" (Hosea 4:8), while Jeremiah said of his contemporary clergymen, "all are greedy for gain . . . all practice deceit" (Jeremiah 6:13).

A survey of ministers in the United States recently conducted by *Leadership* magazine demonstrates that the problem still exists. The survey asked pastors whether, during their ministries, they had ever engaged in sexual activity with someone other than their spouses. Twenty-three percent of those responding said they had.[11] To be sure, most pastors do live lives that are morally sound and somehow make it through their ministries without succumbing to some scandal. But even the best of those who "minister before the Lord" would have to admit to the author's charge that he is "subject to weakness" and regularly has to "offer sacrifices for his own sins, as well as for the sins of the people" (Hebrews 5:2, 3). There is a sense in which all of us who have answered God's call to ministry have been compromised by sin and disqualified by disobedience. Like Israel's priests, we confess that our sin undermines our credibility and hinders our intercessory ministries.

In sharp contrast to the moral turpitude of all the other high priests stands the unimpeachable life of the Son of God. Returning to a theme he has already addressed (cf. Hebrews 4:14—5:10), the author characterizes our high priest as "holy, blameless, pure, set apart from sinners" (Hebrews 7:26). Not compromised by scandal or discredited by hypocrisy, He ministers with complete integrity. Such a high priest "meets our need" because His intercessory ministry is in no way undermined by His own sin. He has the complete confidence of the Father because He ministers before Him "without sin." He also has our confidence because he has truly lived up to His convictions and leads us by His example as well as by His words. Thus, the personal holiness of the Son uniquely qualifies Him to minister on our behalf.

Even so, the superior aspect of Christ's life upon which the author focuses most extensively is not His holiness, but His immortality. The normal career of a priest in Israel was about twenty years (cf. Numbers 8:23, 24). For the high priest, the tenure of service began with the death of the high priest's father and ended with his own

---

[11]*Leadership,* Winter, 1988, pp. 12, 13.

death. In the case of a few high priests, this may have stretched into a period of three or four decades. Inevitably, however, death would end their priesthood.

This is not the case with the priesthood of Christ. The grave, rather than marking the end of His priesthood, marked its beginning. According to the author of Hebrews, the priestly ministry of Christ began with His sacrificial death and continues through His glorious resurrection. Having been "made perfect" through His obedient suffering, He has entered the "heavenly tabernacle" with "his own blood" and has purchased our "eternal redemption." There He continues to intercede before God on our behalf (cf. Hebrews 5:7-10; 7:23-28; 9:11-28).

Among American congregations, long ministries are the exception rather than the rule. While, at times, a change of ministers can prove to be a blessing for all concerned, in most cases it proves to be disruptive and traumatic for minister and congregation alike. The eternal ministry of our great high priest in Heaven, however, provides us with a spiritual constant in an ecclesiastical world of change. Whoever stands before us to minister to Christ's church on earth, there exists beyond and above him a great high priest in Heaven to present us to God.

If this truth be grasped, it has the power to revolutionize our whole concept of the ministry. By realizing that the real "senior minister" of every congregation is Jesus Christ, the church is liberated from some of the undesirable extremes associated with its ministry. A clear vision of Christ as our great high priest can save the church from the "cult of personality" that develops when too much emphasis and authority are given to its human ministers. Artificial and undesirable distinctions between "clergy" and "laity" can begin to melt away. Unrealistic expectations and exploitative demands placed by some churches upon their ministers can be held in check when it is finally realized that the church's earthly ministry is only an expression of a greater and supernatural ministry still being performed by the true "head," the true "high priest" of the church.

This fact, too, can be a great source of comfort to ministers. Ministry consistently rates high in surveys of jobs that generate the greatest amount of stress. This stress has taken its toll on the profession. Of those who "answer the call," more than half change professions within the first ten years. Those who do not "drop out" are likely to "move on." Among American pastors, the average length of ministry with a given congregation is just under two years. A clear concept of Christ as the great high priest of the church can prove to be a great blessing to ministers on the verge of burnout. Pastors who find themselves laboring under the burden of a messiah complex can find release in the fact that the work they have chosen is not theirs alone to do. They are but part of a great redemptive ministry presided over by the true Messiah, who has power and resources that reach far beyond those of His earthly representatives.

So what should a congregation look for first and value most in those it calls to lead its ministry? Without a doubt, the ultimate criterion must be devotion to Jesus Christ as the Son of God and the true high priest of the church. When performed upon Christ's authority, according to His example, and unto His glory, the church's ministry is liberated from its human limitations and is set free to become the very work of God.

CHAPTER ELEVEN

The Trouble With Religion

Hebrews 8:1—9:11

J. Wallace Hamilton tells the story of a preacher who had a most unusual visitor at his church. The morning was hot and stuffy, with little inspiration in it. The congregation was small and sleepy. From behind their waving fans, they looked not too hopefully toward the pulpit, where the preacher, obviously ill-prepared, struggled with his sermon and did not do it very well. It was a totally ineffective performance.

When it was over, he stood at the church door in his usual manner to greet the people as they filed out. There was the usual small talk:

"Hot day, Reverend."

"Yes, dreadful."

"Good morning, Brother Robin; hope it rains."

"Yes, that would be a blessing"; and so on.

Then, suddenly, he was shaking hands with a stranger and something in the eyes and bearing of the man made the preacher uneasy.

"My name is Robin," the preacher said.

"Yes, I know," the man replied.

"And you?"

"It doesn't matter."

"Yes, well we're glad to have you in church. Come again, sir; do come again."

To that invitation, the stranger, with a bewildered look, simply replied, "Why?" Then he turned and walked away.

The preacher did not see any more people after that. Though he continued to shake hands, he did not hear a single word they said. Only one word was in his ears, "Why?"[12] It was the kind of criticism

---

[12]J. Wallace Hamilton, *Where Now Is Thy God?* (Old Tappan: Fleming H. Revell, 1969), p. 91.

every minister dreads, the kind of indictment that shakes a church-man to his very core. It was as if, with a single word, the stranger had invalidated the entire religious enterprise over which the preacher presided; as if he had taken stock of that church and its ministry and judged it unworthy of its calling.

In the text before us, the author of Hebrews is doing the same thing to the religion of Israel. He is taking stock of the cultus of Judaism—its shrine and what went on inside it—and pronouncing it a failure. He walks into the inner sanctum of the religion that the Hebrews had once embraced, takes a long look at the worship practiced there, and then, to the prospect of going back again, he simply replies, "Why?"

What we have here is not some personal vendetta, some mean-spirited desire to get even or put Judaism in its place. Nor is it a condescending critique of religion by some self-proclaimed "expert" on the subject. No, this criticism is born out of love, not anger. It is an expression of concern, not resentment. It owes its origin to an intense, almost desperate, attempt to keep the Hebrews from making a very serious mistake. These Jewish Christians are on the verge of forsaking Christ and "shrinking back" into their former religion. Our author is doing his best to prevent that. Drawing upon all of his powers of persuasion, he attempts to demonstrate logically that the "new and living way" to God provided by faith in Jesus Christ is far superior to the "old" way of Judaism.

Whereas, in the previous section (Hebrews 7:1-28), the author's exposé of Judaism focused upon its priesthood, here the focus is upon Israel's sanctuary and the worship that took place there. Of special interest to the author is the ministry of the high priest in the tabernacle on the Jewish Day of Atonement. It is this ancient liturgical drama, played out in Israel's ancient shrine, that forms the backdrop to the entire line of the argument. We are compelled, therefore, to begin our search for the meaning of this passage with a careful rehearsal of the site and sacraments of Israel's "Most Holy Place."

The Institutions of Jewish Worship

Now the first covenant had regulations for worship and also an earthly sanctuary (Hebrews 9:1).

The Sanctuary

Man's attempts to "show respect for what is sacred" (Latin, *religio*), have given rise to many intriguing and impressive edifices. The mysterious shrines of the Orient, the majestic cathedrals of Europe, the great mosques of the Near East—all stand as compelling examples of the structures man has raised in the name of religion.

Israel, too, had built a house for God. Known to the Hebrews as the Herodian temple of Jerusalem, it existed in its earliest form as the tabernacle—a portable, tentlike structure that served as Israel's first national sanctuary. Called the "tent of meeting" (i.e., where God meets man), the tabernacle was built "according to the pattern" shown to Moses on Mount Sinai (Hebrews 8:5; cf. Exodus 25—27, 35—39). Rather primitive by today's standards, it was designed to suit the semi-nomadic life-style of the early Israelites. It consisted of a wood superstructure covered by curtains of linen and animal skins. Surrounded by a courtyard where the priests offered sacrifice, the tabernacle itself was divided into two rooms, each having furnishings with their own special significance. The chart on the next page will serve to acquaint the reader with the basic arrangement of the tabernacle and its furnishings.

During the forty years of the wilderness wandering, the tabernacle was located at the center of the Israelite camp. On God's signal (the movement of the pillar of cloud), it was dismantled and moved to the site of the next encampment. Following the settlement of Israel in Canaan, the tabernacle was moved from place to place until it was eventually replaced by the permanent structure known as the temple of Solomon. This temple, built according to the basic plan of the tabernacle, was located in Jerusalem and stood at the center of the religious, political, and economic life of the nation. Destroyed by Nebuchadnezzar in 586 B.C., it was eventually rebuilt under the leadership of Zerubbabel (ca. 516 B.C.). The temple with which the Hebrews were familiar was that of Herod the Great (37-4 B.C.), the Roman ruler who remodeled and expanded the temple of Zerubbabel in an effort to win the favor of the Jews. As Jesus predicted (cf. Luke 21:6), this temple, too, was eventually destroyed by Titus in A.D. 70. The early Christians saw in the destruction of the temple and the end of its ritual proof of the validity of Christ's claims to be the Redeemer foreshadowed by the Old Testament ceremonial law. It is this very claim that the author of Hebrews makes from his critique of the tabernacle.

The Sacraments

Among the religious acts performed at the tabernacle, the most important—and the one that receives the greatest attention in the

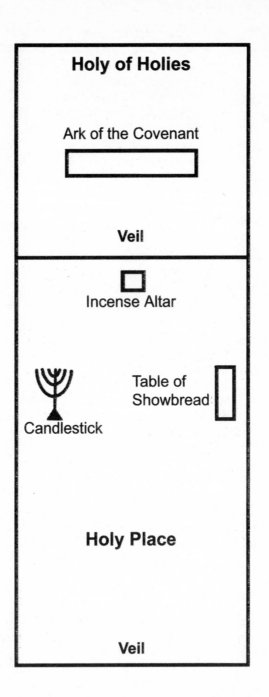

Holy of Holies

Ark of the Covenant

Veil

Incense Altar

Candlestick

Table of
Showbread

Holy Place

Veil

book of Hebrews—is the ministry of the high priest in the Most Holy Place on the Day of Atonement. Each year on the tenth day of the seventh month, the high priest, dressed in linen (a symbol of purity), entered the sacred chamber where the ark of the covenant was located and sprinkled the blood of the sacrificial animal on its lid (known as the "mercy seat" or "atonement cover"). This he did twice, once for his own sin and again for the sins of the people. He then performed another sacrifice, this time applying the blood to the altar of burnt offering outside the tabernacle. Having thus "purged" the sacred precincts of the contamination that came from the "uncleanness and rebellion of the Israelites" (Leviticus 16:16), the high priest turned his attention to a goat ("scapegoat"; Hebrew, *azazel*) that had been especially selected by the casting of lots. Upon the head of this animal he placed his hands, confessing over it "all the wickedness and rebellion of the Israelites." He then ordered it driven away into the wilderness, carrying with it, as it were, "all their sins to a solitary place" (Leviticus 16:20-22).

This annual ritual, coupled with the daily sacrifices performed at the tabernacle, were a constant reminder to the Israelites that the sins they committed were a serious offense to God and disqualified them from coming into His presence. Though the tabernacle and its ministry were designed to grant access to the Holy God by His not-so-holy people, these sacred institutions served actually to underscore how difficult such access is.

The Inadequacy of Jewish Worship

> They serve at a sanctuary that is a copy and shadow of what is in heaven (Hebrews 8:5).

> This is an illustration for the present time, indicating that the gifts and sacrifices being offered were not able to clear the conscience of the worshiper (Hebrews 9:9).

Helmut Thielicke tells the story of a man whose attention was caught by a new sign that appeared in a shop window. It read, "We Do Laundry." Grateful to know that a laundry had opened in his neighborhood, he stopped by one day to patronize the new business. As he stood there before the counter with dirty laundry in hand, an old man, whose clothes were splattered with paint of all colors, came forward and asked him what he wanted. Pointing to the sign he said, "Why, I'd like my laundry cleaned." To that the old man replied, "Mister, you don't understand. We don't do laundry; we paint signs!"

According to the author of Hebrews, this is what the religion of Judaism did. Though the temple and its ministry advertised access to God, it did not really achieve it. Though animal sacrifice addressed the prospect of the forgiveness of sins, it did not really provide for the forgiveness of sins. Far from constituting the very essence of right relationship with God, the temple and its ministry only represented it. At its finest, it was but a "copy," a "shadow," an "illustration" of a higher and greater reality. When it came to the actual business of achieving communion between God and man, the priests who ministered at the temple did not "do laundry," they merely "painted signs."

Even though its construction was commanded by God and was honored by His presence, the tabernacle was yet "man-made" and thereby limited in its capacity to bring man into the presence of the one who made man. Our author focuses upon two of those limitations. The first is one of location. The God of the Bible is not of the earth. He is other than the earth, above the earth, sovereign over the earth. His true abode, His true "throne," is not in the Holy of Holies but in Heaven (Hebrews 8:1). Because the tabernacle was an "earthly sanctuary," it was limited in its ability to provide access to the Heavenly God.

Not only was the sanctuary in the wrong place to provide true access to God, but, as the author goes on to argue, its sacraments were equally incapable of bringing man into God's presence. Designed to remove the sin that stood as a barrier to fellowship with God, "the gifts and sacrifices being offered were . . . only a matter of food and drink and various ceremonial washings—external regulations . . . not able to clear the conscience of the worshiper" (Hebrews 9:9, 10). The whole system of sacrificing animals to atone for human sin was but an "illustration," an anticipation of something "new" that "had not yet been disclosed." It was something God had planned in the long ago and had predicted through the prophet Jeremiah (Jeremiah 31:31-34; cf. Hebrews 8:8-13). He was going to establish a "new covenant" to govern a "new order"—an order characterized by the complete forgiveness of sins and an abiding relationship with God.

This covenant, says the author, is the very one Christ has put into effect through His sacrificial death (Hebrews 9:15-22). What the tabernacle and its ministry could never achieve our great high priest has. He has entered the true tabernacle ("Heaven itself") to minister on our behalf. There, before the very "throne of the Majesty" (Hebrews 8:1), He has offered up "his own blood" to obtain our "eternal redemption" (Hebrews 9:12). Here, at last, is a religion that really works, that provides for true communion between man and God. As the rending of the temple veil at the crucifixion symbolized (Matthew 27:50, 51), Christ has provided us true access to God's "Most Holy Place" (Hebrews 10:19, 20). When we come to God through the ministry of our great high priest, we worship in the one place that can truly be called a "sanctuary." We worship in the very presence of God.

The Implications for Christian Worship

The trouble that the Hebrews were having with Jewish religion is the very trouble that many believers today have with the Christian religion. It is the tendency to confuse the representatives of God with the reality of God; to mistake His emblems for His essence, His symbols for His substance. We get so preoccupied with sacred persons, places, and rituals that we lose sight of the God they represent. In so doing, we turn "intercessors" of man and God into "interveners" between man and God. Instead of using them as a way to God, we allow them to get in the way of God.

The religious institutions of Christianity are not the essence of Christianity. Christ is the essence of Christianity—who He is and what He has done. The structures we build, the clergy we ordain, the theologies we formulate, and the liturgies we perform are at best only a "copy" or a "shadow" of what God is truly like and what it is like to be in His presence. Our religious institutions serve us best when they bring us into that presence and facilitate our worship of the true and living God.

I have a fond memory of a worship experience that succeeded in doing just that. It happened in the old Hopwood Church hard by the banks of Buffalo Creek in Milligan College, Tennessee. I was a first-year seminarian at Emmanuel School of Religion, and twice weekly our seminary family gathered at that little stone church for chapel. Now, as any good seminarian can tell you, chapel services are not always the most inspiring of worship occasions. But this one was different. It was a glorious spring day, full of the grace of God. A larger crowd than usual had assembled and were enthusiastically led into God's presence by a simple but effective liturgy. The guest speaker arose and, treating us just like any other "sinners saved by grace," boldly confronted us with the person of Jesus Christ. Just as he was

95

bringing his sermon to a conclusion, the morning sun cleared the tree line and struck the large stained-glass window located directly behind the pulpit, setting its portrait of the "Good Shepherd" aglow with brilliant color. The benediction was pronounced, and we filed out in profound silence. Something special had happened there, and we all knew it.

Our silence was finally broken by the reverent observation of a wise, old professor, whose very life was itself an act of worship. He said, as if in definition of the very purpose of the Christian religion, "You know, you could hardly see the preacher today for the Christ."

CHAPTER TWELVE

Watch the Lamb

Hebrews 9:11—10:18

In one of his works, songwriter Ray Boltz imagines a Jewish man on his way to Jerusalem to celebrate the Passover, accompanied for the first time by his two small sons. With him he has brought a sacrificial lamb as he has done so many times before. But this Passover is to be different.

Walking on the road to Jerusalem,
   the time had come to sacrifice again.
My two small sons—they walked beside me on the road.
   The reason that they came was to watch the lamb.

"Daddy, Daddy, what will we see there?
   There's so much that we don't understand."
So I told them of Moses and Father Abraham,
   and then I said, "Dear children, watch the lamb."
. . . .
And when we reached the city,
   I knew something must be wrong;
There were no joyful worshipers,
   no joyful worship songs.

I stood there with my children
   in the midst of angry men,
And then I heard the crowd cry out,
   "Crucify Him!"
. . . .
Never have I seen such love
   in any other eyes;
"Into Thy hands I commit My Spirit," He prayed,
   and then He died.

I stood for what seemed like years,
   I'd lost all sense of time—
Until I felt two tiny hands
   holding tight to mine.

. . . .

"Daddy, Daddy, what have we seen here?
   There's so much we don't understand."
So I took them in my arms
   and we turned and faced the cross,
And then I said,
   "Dear children, watch the Lamb."[13]

"Look, the Lamb of God, who takes away the sin of the world!" (John 1:29). Thus John the Baptizer announced the beginning of Jesus' earthly ministry. It seems a strange way to greet Jesus on such an important occasion. Surely he could have chosen more appropriate words. He could have said, "Look, the Son of David who has come to restore the kingdom to Israel!" or, "Look, the Master Teacher, who has come to proclaim the truth of God!" or, "Look, the Great Physician who has come to heal the sick and restore sight to the blind!" or, "Look, the Great Reformer who has come to show us a new way to live!" He might have said all of this, for it is all true. But he reached instead for the very purpose for which Christ had come: "Look, the Lamb of God, who takes away the sin of the world!"

This portion of the book of Hebrews, as clearly as any passage of Scripture, explains just what John's herald meant. Against the backdrop of ancient Jewish ritual, the author portrays the crucifixion of Christ as a sacrifice for sins in an attempt to answer one of the most compelling questions to emerge from the study of Scripture—"Why did Jesus have to die?" Taking us to the foot of the cross, he begins to unfold its meaning as he calls us to "watch the Lamb."

The Background of Jewish Sacrifice

Day after day every priest stands and performs his religious duties; again and again he offers the same sacrifices, which can never take away sins (Hebrews 10:11).

---

[13]"Watch the Lamb," words and music by Ray Boltz. © 1986, Shepherd Boy/ASCAP. All rights reserved. Reprinted by special permission of Diadem Music, Inc., Nashville, Tennessee.

The author's explanation of the meaning of Christ's death begins with a rehearsal of the ancient Israelite ritual of sacrifice. In a procedure that seems most strange to modern Westerners, grains, oil and wine, and domesticated animals were "presented" to God at the altar of the tabernacle (cf. Leviticus 1—7). Offered on different occasions and for different purposes, these gifts and sacrifices stood at the center of ancient Israelite worship. Practiced by all peoples of the ancient Near Eastern world, sacrifices and offerings in the nation of Israel were performed according to a pattern specifically prescribed by God.

In the case of animal sacrifices, an Israelite would bring an unblemished animal from the flock or herd to the altar outside the tabernacle. There he would present the animal to the priest. The worshiper was to place his hands upon the head of the animal so that "it will be accepted on his behalf to make atonement for him" (Leviticus 1:4). The animal was then slain, and its blood was dabbed on the sides of the altar of burnt offering or upon the corners ("horns") of the altar of incense. This special handling of the blood grew out of the concept that the blood is a visible representation of the "life" of the animal designated by God to "make atonement" for the worshiper (Leviticus 17:11). The flesh of the animal was then totally or partially burned upon the altar.

The exact purpose of sacrifice in ancient Israel is difficult to define. Two terms used in the Levitical laws of sacrifice, however, provide us some clues. The first is the term used most frequently to describe the thing presented. It is the word *qorban*, usually translated "offering." The root meaning of this word is "to approach." When used for the "offering," it is best translated "a thing brought near." We may infer from this term and from other language in Leviticus that sacrifice was in some sense a means of approach to God. The author of Hebrews, too, sees this as a function of sacrifice (cf. Hebrews 10:1, 19).

As to how sacrifice provides access to God, another term that is used frequently in the Levitical laws is most instructive. The word is *kipper,* commonly translated "make atonement" in the major versions. Though the precise meaning of this term is debated, it is clear from Leviticus that it has to do with the removal of the consequences of human sin (cf. e.g., Leviticus 4:26, 35; 5:6, 10, 13, 18). According to the Old Testament, sin stands as a barrier between the Holy God and His not-so-holy people. It must be "atoned for" if man is to have access to God. Sacrifice is said to achieve this in two ways: by purifying sin's stain and by paying for sin's debt.[14] Quite appropriately, each of these "illustrations" (cf. Hebrews 9:9) is explored by our author as he presents Christ as the ultimate sacrifice for our sins.

The Blessings of Jesus' Sacrifice

... He entered the Most Holy Place once and for all by his own blood, having obtained eternal redemption (Hebrews 9:12).

How much more, then, will the blood of Christ, who through the eternal Spirit offered himself unblemished to God, cleanse our consciences from acts that lead to death, so that we may serve the living God! (Hebrews 9:14).

The Sacrifice of Christ Pays for Our Sin

Among the many metaphors of sin and its consequences to be found in Scripture, one of the most intriguing is that of sin as "debt." To sin against God is to owe God, to put ourselves in His debt. It is a deep debt, an insurmountable one, the kind we can never get out of by ourselves. Under this debt, we run the risk of losing everything . . . *everything*. "For the wages of sin is death" (Romans 6:23). As long as the debt of our sin remains unpaid, we are under the threat of this ultimate penalty (cf. Ezekiel 18:4).

But God, who is "rich in mercy," makes it possible for us to escape this penalty by offering us an alternative form of payment. In His grace, He is willing to accept another death in the place of our own as "payment" for the debt of sin we owe. Under the law of Moses, this was achieved through sacrifice. In what amounted to an act of "substitution," God was willing to accept the life of the sacrificial victim in the place of the life of the sinner who approached His altar as "compensation" (one of the meanings of Hebrew *koper*, "atonement," which is the equivalent of the Greek *lutron*, translated "redemption" in Hebrews 9:12, and *apolutron*, translated "ransom" in Hebrews 9:15) for the debt His people incurred through sin.

As the author of Hebrews points out, however, the debt of sin was so great and the life of the animal was so inferior to that of the sinner that these sacrifices could never fully "take away sins" (Hebrews 10:1-11). They were at best a provisional payment that temporarily

---

[14]The same two concepts are also joined in Titus 2:14.

delayed the collection of the debt. It is as if God allowed the Israelites to file a Chapter Eleven in lieu of the full payment of their spiritual obligation. And so, day after day, year after year, came the Jews with their sacrifices in an attempt to settle their "accounts." Another sin, another lamb, another payment—the cycle repeated itself until it became obvious that there were not enough lambs in Israel to pay this nagging, ever-accumulating debt.

Until one day, outside Jerusalem, another transaction between man and God took place. This time, the altar was in the form of a cross, and the sacrifice was in the form of a man. He had come to make a final payment ("once for all," Hebrews 7:27; 9:12, 26; 10:12) on the collective spiritual debt of a sinful world. He had come "to give his life as a ransom for many" (Matthew 20:28). And give it He did, in an act of sacrificial love such as the world had never known. Here, at last, was a "payment" of sufficient value, "compensation" of such worth that the Heavenly Creditor said, "Enough! No more! This debt is canceled. It has been paid in full!"

No longer need we cower in fear before God as delinquents before a creditor who is about to repossess our very souls. God has accepted the life of Christ in the place of our own as compensation for the enslaving debt of our sin. "Look, the Lamb of God, who takes away the sin of the world!" . . . Watch the Lamb!

The Sacrifice of Christ Purges Us of Our Sin

In Shakespeare's play *Macbeth*, there is a scene in which Lady Macbeth is observed wandering about in her sleep, struggling with the guilt of her sin. Frantically she rubs her hands, trying to remove the stain of the innocent blood she has conspired to take:

> Out, damned spot! Out, I say!
> . . . .
> What, will these hands ne'er be clean?
> . . . .
> Here's the smell of the blood still: all the perfumes of Arabia will not sweeten this little hand. Oh, oh, oh![15]

We, too, are familiar with that "spot." Sin leaves within us a deep, dark stain that resists our efforts to remove it. Like Pilate before the

---

[15]William H. Shakespeare, *Macbeth*, Act V, Scene I, lines 40-58.

mob, we call for the waters of rationalization in an effort to wash our consciences, to absolve ourselves of guilt. But no matter how hard we scrub, the telltale "spot" remains.

This universal frustration of sinful man was also addressed in the ritual of sacrifice. As an "illustration" of the seriousness of rebellion against God, the Old Testament laws of sacrifice characterized sin as "uncleanness" in need of "purification" (another suggested meaning of the Hebrew *koper*). In the act of sacrifice, the blood of the sacrificial victim was applied as a sort of cleansing agent to the altar (and to the ark of the covenant on the Day of Atonement) to purify it of the individual and collective sins of the Israelites (see, for example, Leviticus 16:15-19). The animal sacrificed had to be "pure" and "without blemish" because, in a symbolic way, its life's blood was being accepted as a "substitute" for the life's blood of the sinner. The life thus taken and the blood thus applied symbolically removed the "uncleanness and rebellion" of Israel, which had soiled God's sanctuary and impeded their access to Him.

But, as the author of Hebrews argues, the "spot" was never permanently removed. It kept reappearing. With each new sin came a new stain in need of cleansing. Day after day, year after year, with sacrifice after sacrifice came the Jews in an effort to remove the stain. Like many religious people in the world today (perhaps even some of us?), they tried by bringing some gift, performing some deed, or participating in some ceremony to purge the guilt of sin from their lives. Like so many modern spiritual pilgrims, they repeatedly stumbled before some "altar" with some "sacrifice" in hand in search of some "priest" who could make them feel forgiven, who could make them feel "clean" again.

The frustration and the futility began to build until one day, "in the fullness of time" ("the time of the new order," Hebrews 9:10), what this ancient ritual could only anticipate and illustrate was finally achieved. A new priest took His place in the sanctuary. He did not simply stand before the altar, He climbed upon it. He did not come to take a life; He came to give one. He did not merely perform the sacrifice; He became the sacrifice.[16]

---

[16]The idea of the high priest's death's being able to atone for wrongdoing is not unknown to the Old Testament. According to Numbers 35:25-32 and Joshua 20:6, the manslayer who had been exiled to a city of refuge was allowed to go free upon the death of the high priest.

"Look, the Lamb of God, who takes away the sin of the world." We do not understand the cross until we see it as an altar where the Son of God voluntarily died in our place, where the Lamb of God gave His blood to pay for our sins—to wash our sins away. The prophet Isaiah anticipated the substitutionary atonement of Christ in his moving portrait of the suffering servant. Hear it well, for it speaks as clearly as any passage of Scripture of what Jesus did for you and me:

> But he was pierced for our transgressions,
>   he was crushed for our iniquities;
> the punishment that brought us peace was upon him,
>   and by his wounds we are healed.
>
> We all, like sheep, have gone astray,
>   each of us has turned to his own way;
> and the Lord has laid on him the iniquity of us all.
>
> He was oppressed and afflicted,
>   yet he did not open his mouth;
> He was led like a lamb to the slaughter,
>   and as a sheep before her shearers is silent,
>   so he did not open his mouth.
>
> By oppression and judgment he was taken away.
>   And who can speak of his descendants?
> For he was cut off from the land of the living;
>   for the transgression of my people he was stricken.
>
> He was assigned a grave with the wicked,
>   and with the rich in his death,
> though he had done no violence,
>   nor was any deceit in his mouth.
>
> Yet it was the Lord's will to crush him and cause him to suffer,
>   and though the Lord makes his life a guilt offering,
> he will see his offspring and prolong his days,
>   and the will of the Lord will prosper in his hand.
>
> After the suffering of his soul,
>   he will see the light of life and be satisfied;

by his knowledge my righteous servant will justify many,
    and he will bear their iniquities.
Therefore I will give him a portion among the great,
    and he will divide the spoils with the strong,
because he poured out his life unto death,
    and was numbered with the transgressors.

For he bore the sin of many,
and made intercession for the transgressors (Isaiah 53:5-12).

The message of the cross is that, in the sacrificial death of Jesus Christ, God has done for us what we could never do for ourselves. In an incomprehensible expression of love, God has acted to right the wrong we have committed against Him. He has offered up His own Son to "take away" the consequences of our sin. The blood of the Lamb has removed sin's stain, and His death has paid sin's debt. We are, at last, cleansed and set free to serve the living God! (Hebrews 9:14, 15).

"Look, the Lamb of God, who takes away the sin of the world." If you wish to see the cross for what it was, how great the love that wrought it, how great the forgiveness that it achieved—"watch the Lamb!" If you desire to be rid of the dark stain that soils your conscience, pollutes your personality and sullies your self-esteem—"watch the Lamb!" If you seek freedom from the great debt that robs you of your joy and threatens the repossession of your very soul—"watch the Lamb!" If you wish to understand why Jesus had to die—"watch the Lamb!"

CHAPTER THIRTEEN

Finishing What We Start

Hebrews 10:19-39

Edmund Steinle was one of the great preachers of his day. Each week, thousands of people heard him speak at the major metropolitan church where he ministered and over his radio program, which was aired throughout most of America. One spring, his preaching dipped perceptively, and privately he even contemplated leaving the ministry. But, by fall, he had regained his form and seemed driven by a new resolve and a new sense of calling. One Sunday, he explained to his congregation just what had happened. He had lost his wife that spring, and the darkness of that time nearly drove him away from the faith and into the black pit of total despair. But one night, as he stood on the precipice of apostasy, he had a "conversation" with God. He accused God of unfairly taking his wife and then asked God to give him one good reason to "finish the course" of the Christian life. He waited for God's answer, expecting a deep theological treatise in King James English. Instead he seemed to get a simple word of challenge and encouragement, the kind that can be heard only through the ears of faith. "Hang in there, Edmund," God seemed to say. "Hang in there."

In a sense, that is what God is saying to these Hebrew Christians. Here is a church that, in the words of Fred Craddock, has "lost its 'Amen.'"[17] But, instead of getting down on all fours in search of it, they just do not seem to care. Life's injustices have knocked the fight right out of them, and they are ready to throw in the towel. Some loving pastor, who knows them well and cares for them deeply, comes now with words of encouragement and warning, desperately trying to save them from an act of apostasy that could have

---

[17]Fred Craddock, *The Recorded Sermons of Fred Craddock* (Atlanta: Emory University, 1986).

irreversible and eternal consequences. This is more than theology; it is an impassioned plea. "Hold on!" encourages the author. "Stand your ground! Don't give up! Persevere! Hang in there, Hebrew Christians. Hang in there!"

This powerful call to perseverance is made from three different perspectives, each of which has been explored in the author's previous argument and is relevant to the actual circumstances of his readers. We will consider them here in the same order as they appear in the text.

The Certainties of Faith in Christ

> Therefore, brothers, since we have confidence to enter the Most Holy Place by the blood of Jesus . . . let us draw near to God with a sincere heart in full assurance of faith . . . (Hebrews 10:19, 22).

In one of his novels, George Moore tells of Irish peasants back during the Great Depression who were put to work by the government building roads. For a while, they worked well, singing their glad Irish songs. But gradually, they began to discover that the roads they were building led nowhere. They ran out in uninhabited bogs and isolated glens. This discovery broke their spirit. They soon lost all enthusiasm for their work. What had once been a purposeful pursuit became a drudgery and a chore. Moore made this observation: "The roads to nowhere are difficult to make. For a man to work well and sing, there must be an end in view."

And so it is in the Christian life. One of the keys to the successful completion of our spiritual pilgrimage is the confidence that there is a worthwhile destination at its end. "The roads to nowhere are difficult to make." It is hard to generate the drive and energy necessary for faithful Christian living without confidence of some eventual arrival, of some final consummation of the journey. For a Christian to "work well and sing, there must be an end in view."

Aware of this, our author begins his call to perseverance with an affirmation of a certain expectation that all Christians enjoy through the redemptive ministry of Jesus Christ. Through Christ, he says, we have assurance of access to God. We do not have to make our pilgrimage burdened by the fear that we might strive our best to reach Heaven's gate only to be denied entrance when we finally arrive. One of the great messages of the book of Hebrews is that, if we seek salvation through Jesus Christ, we will find it. "Have confidence in that," the author says, "count on it; stake your eternal destiny on it."

"Draw near to God with a sincere heart in full assurance of faith" (Hebrews 10:22).

For the Christian, there is an "end in view" and the hope of that end has served to motivate believers to faithfulness throughout the centuries. This faith in a "grand finale," in which commitment will be rewarded and life's tragedies will be explained, has enabled the persecuted to persevere in the face of insurmountable odds. It is the hope to which Ivan, in *The Brothers Karamazov,* kept returning:

> I believe like a child that suffering will be healed and made up for, that in the world's finale something so precious will come to pass that it will suffice for all our hurts, for the comforting of our resentments, for the atonement of all the crimes of humanity. . . . I want to be there when everyone suddenly understands what it has all been for.[18]

"Hold on to your hope," says our author. Why? Because hope will ultimately be realized at the end of the Christian life. The assurance of access to the Heavenly sanctuary that lies at our journey's end empowers our pilgrimage to God's "Most Holy Place." We endure the rigors of the "straight and narrow" way because we know there is Someone waiting at the other end—Someone who loves us and who, because of the sacrifice of Jesus Christ, is willing to receive us unto himself.

Not only does this assurance of arrival empower Christians to keep going in the face of life's tragedies, it also motivates them to do Christ's work on earth. A Christian's confidence in the future should never result in lack of concern for the present. The prospect of our eternal life in Heaven should never translate into a socially irresponsible faith that looks at this earthly existence as merely a time to wait, a place to bide our time until "the Day approaches." It should rather, as our author insists, lead us to "consider how we may spur one another on toward love and good deeds" (Hebrews 10:24). Our appreciation of the redemption Christ has achieved for us and the destiny He has secured for us should generate within us a sacrificial desire to minister in His name and on His behalf. The love we offer and the good deeds we do are made more meaningful by the realization that they make a real contribution to a great redemptive

---

[18]Feodor Dostoyevsky, *The Brothers Karamazov,* tr. by Constance Garnett (New York: Grosset & Dunlap, 1949), p. 733.

enterprise that will find its consummation in Heaven. For those who tend to think of Christian hope as a barrier to vital Christian ministry to the needs of the world, the observation of C.S. Lewis should prove most instructive. In his book *Christian Behaviour,* he observes: "If you read history you will find that the Christians who did the most for the present world were those who thought the most of the next."

For the Christian, life is more than existence. It is journey, it is progress toward a glorious destiny. It is a pilgrimage made with the confidence that something of ultimate consequence lies at its end. The assurance of hope blesses us at journey's end and all along the way. Indeed, it is one of those things that calls us back from the brink of apostasy, that encourages us to finish what we have started, that enables us to "hang in there."

The Consequences of Forsaking Christ

> If we deliberately keep on sinning after we have received the knowledge of the truth, no sacrifice for sins is left, but only a fearful expectation of judgment and of raging fire that will consume the enemies of God (Hebrews 10:26, 27).

If there were ever a "hard saying" of Scripture, then certainly this is it. For the second time in his letter (cf. Hebrews 6:4-8), the author raises the prospect of a believer's regressing beyond a "point of no return" in his spiritual life. Here the author warns believers of sinning against God to the point that they have no prospect of restoration, but "only a fearful expectation of judgment."

As one might imagine, this passage (Hebrews 10:26-31) has received a great deal of attention from the interpreters, many of whom seek to understand it from the viewpoint of a certain theological system. Those who will not admit to the possibility of a believer's "falling from grace" tend to explain the text as referring either to a judgment of those who were not "true believers" or to a "chastening" of sinful believers that, though it may be to the point of physical death, yet still falls short of the actual forfeiture of eternal salvation. On the other hand, there are those who contend that this text teaches that a single post-baptismal sin leads to the irrevocable forfeiture of the believer's salvation. Other attempted explanations fall somewhere in between, often focusing upon some particular aspect of the text. Some interpreters insist, for example, that the key to the meaning is to be found in the idea of sinning "deliberately" (as opposed to "ignorantly" or "inadvertently"; cf. Hebrews 5:2) and compare the text to Numbers 15:27-31, which, it is argued, teaches that "unintentional" sins could be forgiven through sacrifice, but that "defiant" sins could not. Others suggest that the meaning of the passage should be sought in the words *keep on sinning,* which, it is argued, mean that only a "repeated, habitual" sin or a "life-style" of sin threatens the believer with the forfeiture of salvation.

While there may be an element of truth in some of these suggestions, a more useful approach is one that seeks to define the entire clause, *if we deliberately keep on sinning,* in light of the immediate and larger context of the book. The author tells us exactly what kind of offense he has in mind in the verses that follow. The believer worthy of God's judgment is one "who has trampled the Son of God under foot, who has treated as an unholy thing the blood of the covenant that sanctified him, and who has insulted the Spirit of grace" (Hebrews 10:29). He is referring to those who "throw away [their] confidence" (Hebrews 10:35), who "shrink back and are destroyed," as compared to those "who believe and are saved" (Hebrews 10:39). The sin he is describing here is what he earlier called "crucifying the Son of God all over again and subjecting him to public disgrace" (Hebrews 6:6) and having "a sinful, unbelieving heart that turns away from the living God" (3:12).

It is clear here that the author is not speaking of mere human weakness or inclination to sin. In fact, he has already assured his readers that the priestly ministry of Christ helps us with those temptations and assists us when we go astray (Hebrews 2:18; 4:16; 5:2). No, the "sin" he has in mind here is not the moral stumbling of a struggling Christian. It is the sin of "apostasy." It is abandonment of faith in Jesus Christ. It is the "deliberate" rejection of the salvation that God has provided in Christ's sacrificial death. More than an act of sin, it is a state of sin, a way of life by which a believer deliberately abandons his relationship with Christ and persistently repudiates the salvation of God in Christ. Our author, as John Calvin says, is "directing his attention . . . to those who desert Christ in their unbelief and so deprive themselves of the benefit of his death."

If this be grasped, then the author's claim that for such a one "no sacrifice for sins is left" (Hebrews 10:26) is also understood. In other words, if we reject the redemption that God offers in the sacrificial death of Jesus Christ, there simply is no other provision for our forgiveness. What God did in Christ, He did "once and for all." To forsake Christ, then, is to forfeit humanity's only hope for salvation.

Lest anyone should miss the grave seriousness of abandoning faith in Christ, our author concludes this section with a stern reminder of God's capacity to punish those who defy Him, warning, "It is a dreadful thing to fall into the hands of the living God" (Hebrews 10:31).

To some people, the idea of an angry, vengeful God who punishes humans for their sins is simply unacceptable. In a culture where we have lost the will to hold ourselves and one another accountable for our actions, it is difficult to conceive of a God who does. The God of modern man is a Heavenly patsy who is soft on crime and a sucker for a sob story. He is a cosmic caterer who exists to dispense health and wealth to humankind. Ironically, irresponsible churchmen have contributed to these modern misconceptions of God by creating a theological climate in which grace is viewed as a moral loophole and mercy as an invitation to ethical irresponsibility. To a world that knows how to get what it wants, such a God is the ultimate pushover, an easy mark for unscrupulous manipulation.

The author of Hebrews joins a chorus of New Testament writers who refute this unbalanced and inaccurate portrait of God. Quoting from the Old Testament, he reminds his readers that "the Lord will judge His people" (Hebrews 10:30; cf. Deuteronomy 32:36; Psalm 135:14). Yes, God is a God of love, but He is also a God of wrath. This is as true in the New Testament as it is in the Old. Any theology that does not take both of these aspects of His nature into account is simply not Biblically accurate. If we follow Christ, we may approach the thought of drawing near to God with "confidence" and "full assurance." Should we forsake Christ, however, turn our backs on Him and abandon our relationship with Him, we should approach the thought of facing Him with utmost fear and dread. Jesus Christ is God's very Son, whom He has personally sent to die that we might be forgiven of our sins. It is the clear warning of this text that, should a Christian deliberately and persistently turn his back on this unspeakable gift, he should expect nothing less than the terrifying wrath of God.

J.P. McEvoy, a *Reader's Digest* roving editor, used to tell about the time he went to London and decided to visit an English court of law to observe British justice in action. The case being tried was one of wife-beating, with the wife as chief witness. She graphically described her husband's brutality, but, at the last minute, she had a change of heart. "I wish to withdraw my complaint, your lordship," she said to the judge. "I find no fault with this man." His lordship looked grimly down from the bench. "England does!" he said, and proceeded to pass sentence anyway.

Though we may pronounce ourselves and one another "innocent" of wrong, there is another verdict that must be heard. It comes from the only true and righteous Judge, and it is this sentence that ultimately matters. Upon it hangs our eternal destinies, and, in view of it, we should respectfully live.

The Cost of Following Christ

> You need to persevere so that when you have done the will of God, you will receive what he has promised (Hebrews 10:36).

The Christian businessman S. Truett Cathy once described how God blesses the perseverance of the faithful Christian:

> I believe God wants us to be successful . . . and yet success is not always obvious. The Chinese bamboo tree does absolutely nothing—or so it seems—for the first four years. Then suddenly, sometime during the fifth year, it shoots up ninety feet in sixty days. Would you say that bamboo tree grew in six weeks, or five years? I think our lives are akin to the Chinese bamboo tree. Sometimes we put forth effort, put forth effort, and put forth effort . . . and nothing seems to happen. But if you do the right things long enough, you'll receive the rewards of your efforts.[19]

In a sense, this is the message of this portion of the book of Hebrews. The book of Hebrews views the Christian life as a spiritual pilgrimage driven by the deep conviction that our efforts to live for Christ will eventually be vindicated. Christ has personally secured a successful end to our journey through His sacrificial death and glorious resurrection. What He asks of us is simply to persevere, to keep doing the right thing, to follow Christ to the journey's end.

The Christian life is not a sprint. It is a distance run. To complete it successfully, you do not have to be a spiritual superstar, one of those gifted people who always seems to be setting records in traditional piety, making great plays and piling up personal bests in the arena of religious achievement. You do not even have to be morally perfect, winning every battle with temptation and achieving absolute ethical purity.

---

[19]S. Truett Cathy, quoted in *Leadership,* Summer, 1986, p. 35.

What you have to do, says our author, is to stay in the race. Sure, you are going to face obstacles. Sure, you are going to get tired and discouraged. Sure, you are going to stumble. But don't give up! Keep running! Persevere! Hang in there! Fix your eyes on Christ. Keep yourself on course. Go the distance. For in the marathon of the Christian life, "the race is not to the swift," but to the steadfast. The victory belongs not to the fast, but to the faithful, to those who finish the race.

It is a message the Hebrews needed to hear. If they had accepted Christ with some grand vision of how easy and rewarding life with Him was going to be, by now that illusion has been shattered. By now, they have personally discovered what Dwight L. Moody, the great evangelist, also came to realize. Soon after his conversion he wrote:

> When I was converted, I made this mistake: I thought the battle was already mine, the victory already won, the crown already in my grasp. I thought the old things had passed away, that all things had become new, and that my old corrupt nature, the old life, was gone. But I found out, after serving Christ for a few months, that conversion was only like enlisting in the army—that there was a battle on hand.[20]

For the Hebrews, that "battle" has taken its toll. For a while, they faithfully "stood [their] ground in a great contest in the face of suffering" (Hebrews 10:32). But now they are beginning to tire. They have reached the place in the "race" that marathoners call "the wall," that place where energy has been totally depleted and fatigue sets in, and the runner, feeling he lacks the strength to finish, wants to quit. They have been brought to their "wall" by persecution. It has come in the form of insult, the confiscation of their property, and imprisonment. They have gone far enough with Christ to learn, with Thomas 'A Kempis, that "If thou bear the cross, it will soon bear thee." Now, some of them are wanting to climb off that cross and to drop out of the race.

John Claypool is a man who once thought of dropping out of the race. Early in his ministry, his little daughter developed leukemia. Just like so many other parents who have had their hearts broken by this dreaded disease, he and his wife went through the cruel cycle of

---

[20]*Leadership,* Summer, 1982, p. 92.

diagnoses, remission, recurrence and finally loss of someone more precious than life itself. When his daughter died, something died in John Claypool. He got disoriented in his grief, lost his spiritual equilibrium and contemplated dropping out of the race. He could not preach for the longest time. Somehow the pious platitudes that he had once spouted to others now seemed empty and inadequate.

Late one night, in search of the strength to go on, his eyes lighted upon Isaiah 40:31 as though reading it for the very first time:

> But those who hope in the Lord will renew their strength. They will soar on wings like eagles; they will run and not grow weary, they will walk and not be faint.

That promise of Scripture turned John Claypool around. It became the text of the first sermon he preached upon his return to the pulpit. He said that he had finally learned from life what this text had said all along—that God's strength comes in different forms, each one appropriate to the specific needs of His children. Sometimes God's strength comes in the form of ecstasy. It gives us the ability to "soar on wings" of spiritual exhilaration. At other times, it supplies us with energy. It fills us with the resolve and drive to "run and not grow weary," to accomplish some great work, to see some task through to its completion. But, as he had come to learn, there are times in life when ecstasy is impossible and energy is useless. There are some things over which you cannot soar, and about which you can do absolutely nothing. So what does a struggling saint do when he cannot fly and when he cannot run? He walks. He puts one foot in front of the other, takes one step after another and simply keeps moving. With all he holds dear crumbling around him, he clings tenaciously to his faith, and he just "hangs in there."[21]

Now to some, the power to endure is the lowest form of God's strength. In fact, some say that Isaiah had it all wrong. He got these phrases out of order. As any good student of rhetoric can tell you he should have saved his best to last. He should have begun with "walking," moved on to "running," and ended with "soaring." After all, is not ecstasy, spiritual exhilaration, the greatest form of God's "strength"? Maybe not. Who is to say but that, in the final analysis, the greatest form of God's strength is simply the ability to endure, to

---

[21]John R. Claypool, *The Tracks of a Fellow Struggler* (Waco: Word, 1982).

persevere in the face of suffering, to hold on in the face of discouragement, to keep the faith, to finish what we have started?

> When we have exhausted our store of endurance,
> When our strength has failed ere the day is half done,
> When we reach the end of our hoarded resources,
> Our Father's full giving is only begun.
>
> Annie Johnson Flint

Hang in there, Christian. Hang in there!

CHAPTER FOURTEEN

The Field of Faith

Hebrews 11:—12:3

Field of Dreams, the award-winning film by Phil Alden Robinson, is the story of one man's determination to follow his "dream" no matter how absurd it seems or how much it costs him. While walking in the cornfields of his Midwestern farm, Ray Kinsella hears a voice from an invisible source. "If you build it, he will come," it says. Unsure of the meaning of this commission, Ray is yet convinced that it calls him to a pursuit of ultimate importance. As his commitment to the dream deepens, he receives new clues to its meaning. He realizes that it is a baseball diamond that he must build—a field to which players from the past can return to realize their dreams and fulfill their unfinished careers.

Seeming to abandon all reason, he puts his farm at risk of foreclosure, plows up several acres of prime farmland, and spends his life's savings to build his "field of dreams." As promised, the baseball greats of the past begin to appear, though they are visible only to those who share the dream. There is "Shoeless Joe" Jackson, a member of the notorious Chicago Black Sox team that was accused of throwing the 1919 World Series. Though it was never proved that Jackson was involved in the scandal, he suffered the same fate as several of his teammates and was banished from the game he loved at the very height of his outstanding career. There is the "Iron man," Lou Gehrig, struck down in his prime by the disease that now bears his name. And there is the mysterious "Doc" Braden, who played but one inning of major-league ball before leaving the game to become a physician.

One by one they appear, each with his own story to tell. Ray is inspired by their play, and he receives great satisfaction from knowing that his sacrificial pursuit of his dream has made it possible for them to fulfill theirs. Through it all, he is beset by a certain restlessness—frustrated by the prospect that, although his obedience to the "voice" has benefited others, it will not result in anything of lasting benefit to him.

"Finish it and he will come," urges the voice. It is not until Ray himself steps onto the field that he understands what it has all been for. For there to greet him is another "player" from the past. It is someone he once knew, someone he had wronged, someone from whom he desperately needed forgiveness. It is his father, long deceased, now reappearing to offer reconciliation. The movie ends with father and son reunited by a simple game of catch while people from far and wide stream to the field of dreams in search of their own fulfillment.

"Finish it and he will come." The message Ray Kinsella received in an Iowa cornfield is not all that different from the one our author is here delivering to the Hebrew Christians. Employing an athletic motif, the author places the Hebrews on a field of faith, fills the grandstands with the spiritual giants of the past, and urges these struggling Christians to follow their dream to its conclusion, to complete the "race" of the Christian life, no matter how absurd it may seem or how much it may cost. In the process, he teaches them what it means to live by faith.

A Description of the Life of Faith

Now faith is being sure of what we hope for and certain of what we do not see (Hebrews 11:1).

This famous verse is not so much a definition of faith as it is a description of how faith expresses itself in life. As A. B. Bruce says in his classic commentary on Hebrews, "The main purpose of this discourse is not to show the abstract nature of faith, but its moral power: how it enables men to live noble lives and so gain a good report."[22] This passage is not so much about belief in spite of evidence as it is about life in scorn of consequences.

The "faith" described here is the equivalent of what we might call a "life perspective." It is about a sense of assurance that Christians have that the spiritual is superior to the material and that the eternal is superior to the temporal. It is about a life-shaping conviction that the promises of God in Christ, though of things "not seen" and "yet

---

[22]A. B. Bruce, *The Epistle to the Hebrews* (Edinburgh: T. & T. Clark, 1899), p. 412.

to come," are absolutely true and will be ultimately realized. It is what the author elsewhere calls "hope," much as Paul describes it in the book of Romans:

> But hope that is seen is no hope at all. Who hopes for what he already has? But if we hope for what we do not yet have, we wait for it patiently (Romans 8:24).

"Certain of what we do not see and sure of what is yet to come"—many find it difficult to live by such a code. In an age of the electron microscope and chemical analysis, we are more inclined to follow what we can empirically prove and logically conclude than what we can bring ourselves to believe. Modern Westerners come from Missouri—"Show me" is the motto of our lives. Like Thomas of old, we will believe only if we can see the nail prints in His hands. Approaching the mystery of God like an algebra problem: we try to "solve" Him with a slide rule and a calculator. If we can squeeze Him into a logical equation and assign a value to every "unknown," we might just be willing to conclude that He is. How God must smile from Heaven!

In the face of this skepticism and empiricism, the Bible insists that the ultimate reality in the material universe is not material at all. He is "Eternal Spirit"—imperceptible to the senses and unintelligible to the mind. Though He has manifested himself to us in creation, disclosed himself to us in history, expressed himself to us in the Scriptures, and revealed himself to us in His Son, He is yet other than us and beyond us—of a higher reality that transcends the physical world and the ways we can comprehend it. His existence cannot be verified, proved, or substantiated. It can only be believed. The door to His world cannot be opened by the perception of our senses, the logic of our minds, or the tools of our sciences. It is only opened by faith: "anyone who comes to him must *believe* that he exists and that he rewards those who earnestly seek him" (Hebrews 11:6).

The "faith" (Greek, *pistis*) of which our author speaks is more than a conclusion of the mind—some assent to an assertion or verdict upon a body of evidence. It is also a conviction of the "heart"—a confidence that God is who He claims to be and will do what He says He will do. To "believe" (Greek, *pisteuo*) in God is to trust God, to take Him at His word. At its finest, it is to rely upon God and submit to Him unto salvation and eternal life. It is to surrender to life's ultimate reality in view of life's ultimate concern.

A Demonstration of the Life of Faith

By faith Noah . . . built an ark. . . . Abraham . . . offered Isaac. . . . Moses . . . chose to be mistreated. . . . Others were tortured and . . . put to death. . . . The world was not worthy of them (Hebrews 11:7-40).

Therefore, since we are surrounded by such a great cloud of witnesses . . . let us run with perseverance the race marked out for us. Let us fix our eyes on Jesus, the author and perfecter of our faith . . . (Hebrews 12:1, 2).

It is said that, when Napoleon Bonaparte began his Egyptian campaign, he pointed to the pyramids and shouted to his men, "Soldiers, forty centuries look down upon you!" In a sense, this is what the author of Hebrews is saying to these struggling Christians. "Your contest of faith is not going unnoticed," he tells them. "It is being witnessed by a grandstand full of former contestants, whose careers of faith ended without ever receiving 'what had been promised,' but who faithfully finished their course of faith. It is now your turn to do the same."

It is an interesting crowd that the author has assembled in the stands. Some of these inductees to the Religious Hall of Fame were not exactly what you would call moral giants. There's that "deceiver," Jacob, who cheated his brother out of his birthright and tricked his dying father. There's Samson, that ill-tempered rogue who was always looking for a fight. There's the fair-haired David whose voyeurism led to adultery and murder. There's father Abraham, who, to save his own skin, pretended that his wife was his sister and allowed her to be taken into another man's harem. There's impetuous Jepthah, whose rash vow cost his daughter her life. There's Rahab—we all know what kind of woman she was. One thing's for sure. These people did not get invited to this event because they were morally perfect.

Then why did they get invited? What was it that they did that was so special, so worthy of emulation? What is it that they all have in common and to which the Hebrews should aspire? The answer is that they all did something noteworthy "by faith." In a moment of truth, they valued the spiritual over the material, prized the eternal more than the temporal and acted on faith and faith alone. For Noah, it was building a boat to escape a flood that did not come for more than a hundred years. For Abraham, it was a willingness to kill the very son whom God had promised and in whom his whole future rested, for no other reason than simply that God said so. For Moses, it was a decision to give up the royal palace for the slave pit because he regarded kinship with God's people more important than kingship over their oppressors. For Rahab, it was a bold willingness to side with the Israelite invaders rather than with her fellow-citizens in Jericho because she had come to believe in the power of Israel's God. Name after name, right on down the list—every one of them accomplished something significant or endured something difficult out of faith and faith alone. In spite of timely problems and in view of timeless possibilities, they managed "by faith" to do the right thing. Refusing to be discouraged by their failures or to be disqualified by their flaws, they found some way to be faithful, to run another lap, to stay in the race. Now they are in the stands, cheering for the Hebrews.

"These were all commended for their faith," says the author, "yet none of them received what had been promised" (Hebrews 11:39). They did what they did without seeing their faith vindicated or their faithfulness rewarded. They lived their lives "by faith" rather than "by sight," by what they were promised rather than by what they could perceive. Any Christian not prepared to do the same, is not prepared to live by faith.

"We are surrounded by a great cloud of witnesses." The list of names is impressive, and it continues to grow. Stephen, Paul, Joan of Arc, Livingston—the grandstands continue to fill with those who have lived and died "by faith." "The world was not worthy of them." And neither are we. I tell you, it is hard to quit with people like that looking on. Just about the time we think we have endured all we can endure and have given all that we can give, we catch a glimpse of someone who has given far more, and we decide to run just one more lap. Maybe it is an exhausting struggle with some sin we have committed. It is so terrible that we feel that we will never be able to live it down. It disqualifies us, makes us feel like we do not even belong on the "field." But just as we are about to quit, David stands up, and then Peter. "It's all right," they say. "We know how you feel. But don't let it stop you. God forgave us. He has forgiven you. Keep running." And, somehow, we know that we can. Or maybe things just have not been going well lately. In fact, life seems to be falling apart. We seem to be losing everything we hold dear and are beginning to think that God has abandoned us. Maybe what they are saying is right. Maybe we are being punished for some terrible sin.

Maybe we ought to give up. Maybe we ought just to "curse God and die." But then we hear a voice from the stands. It is Job. "You can make it," he says. "Keep going." And somehow we know that we can. Or maybe the price of discipleship is getting too high to pay. It is forcing us to reorder some of our priorities, to give up some things we really want to do. We are trying to do the right thing, but all we get is grief. Our faith is closing some doors against us, alienating us from some important people. People are looking for ways to discredit us, and some of our best "friends" have begun to betray us. But just when we are about to "bail," to "throw in the towel," Jeremiah stands up and shouts, "You can do it! You can see it through to the end." And somehow we know that we will.

Maybe you have another name to add to the list—a preacher, a parent, a Sunday-school teacher, a friend—your own hero from the past whose career of faith inspires you to go on. Mine is a woman named Lois. As people are commonly measured, she achieved little and accumulated even less. She only went as far as the tenth grade in school and worked most of her life as a clerk in a grocery store. When she died, her estate consisted of a small mobile home, some dishes, a photo album, and a 1957 Rambler. Her entire life was "spent" putting other people first and doing the things nobody else wanted to do. She was, without a doubt, the best person I ever knew. Hers is the first face I look for in the crowded stands when I step onto my field of faith. Not a few times the sound of her cheers have kept me in the race. She always sits in the upper deck, last row, in the corner—the "nosebleed" section, so high and far away from the action that the contestants look like ants. It is not so much that she likes those seats. She just likes to see other people get the better ones. There she sits, a mile away from the action, still somehow managing to pick me out of the large field of contestants and personally cheer me on.

She's not easy to spot. She "roots" the same way she used to "run"—inconspicuously and unpretentiously—somewhere in the middle of the pack. She'll probably be surrounded by a crowd of squirming kids, children from the neighborhood on whom she has spent her last dollar to buy tickets so they could see their first race. There she'll be, right in the middle of them, trying to watch the race while she passes out popcorn and wipes runny noses.

She was good in her day, this veteran runner. She could have gone far in her sport. But, somehow, she never seemed quite able to pull off a win. Instead, she was always getting distracted by what was going on around her. It was almost as if the needs of the other runners were more important than where she finished in the field. Some competitor, huh? She had run some hard races in her life . . . hard races, the kind that break a lot of people. But she never complained and, most importantly, she never quit. Her career of faith, triumphant and heroic, was tragically cut short by an "injury." "Cancer," they said. "Inoperable," they said; and in a few months she was gone.

For a while there, after her death, I lost my will to compete. In fact, I even considered dropping out of the sport all together. But one of the "coaches" of my fallen hero interrupted my self-pity one day with the most effective pep talk I ever received. "Steve," he said, "you know your mother took great joy in your work for the Lord." And so she did. And, if I understand this passage from Hebrews correctly, she still does. For somewhere up in the stands, up there with Abraham and Sarah and Priscilla and Paul, sits another saint—cheering me on, shouting her encouragement, urging me to run with perserverance the race that is set before me. Somehow— and it will be "by faith"—I am going to finish this race. I don't care how hard it gets or how much it is going to take out of me, I am not going to let that lady down.

CHAPTER FIFTEEN

Loved by Perfection

Hebrews 12:4-13

The virtuoso sits at the piano and begins to play. As the concert progresses, the master seems to attack the instrument, pouncing upon its keys with all his might, pushing the instrument to its physical limits as if in an effort to squeeze out of it every resonant sound that it possesses, the best that it has to give, refusing to quit until its lovely song is set free to echo throughout the hall. It is hard to be loved by perfection.

The master sculptor furiously chips away at the large piece of marble in his studio. The room is full of dust and debris; the air reverberates with the ring of the hammer and the shrill whine of the grinder as the artist pounds, then polishes, his rough stone, determined to summon forth the thing of beauty that hides within it. It is hard to be loved by perfection.

Even so, says the author of Hebrews, does the Creator love His creatures. Like a devoted Father who wants what is best both for and from His children, He lays His hand upon our lives, determined to see us rise to our spiritual potential. At times, the Father's affection for His children expresses itself in His correction of His children. When it does, we learn, along with the Hebrews, that it is hard to be loved by perfection.

The Father's Affection for His Children

The Lord disciplines those he loves . . . (Hebrews 12:6).

God is treating you as sons . . . (Hebrews 12:7).

The Bible paints many portraits of God and how He relates to humankind. He is the Creator and we are His creatures, made in His image and in His likeness. He is the Sovereign and we are His subjects, summoned to submit to His supreme authority. He is the Good

Shepherd and we are His sheep, called to follow Him for provision and protection. Each of these metaphors reveals some aspect of God's nature and some dimension of the dynamics by which He interacts with human beings.

But the greatest Biblical model of the divine-human encounter is that of a Father to His children. God is the commanding Father, dictating His wishes to His children (Deuteronomy 14:1ff). He is the protective Father, rescuing His children from peril and shielding them from harm (Exodus 4:22-23; Deuteronomy 1:31). He is the providing Father, responding generously to the requests of His children (Luke 11:1-13). He is the broken-hearted Father, hurt and bewildered by the rebellion of His children (Isaiah 1:2, 3). He is the angry Father, whose patience has been exhausted and who is determined to punish His recalcitrant children (Deuteronomy 32:5-22). He is the forgiving Father, longsuffering toward His wayward children, eagerly awaiting their return (Luke 15:11-32). Not only is God uniquely the Father of Jesus, He is also, in a very real sense, "Our Father in heaven" (Matthew 6:9).

The Biblical metaphor of the fatherhood of God owes its origin to the nature of the society from which God first chose a people for himself. The peoples of Biblical times lived their lives as part of an extended family—a tribe or clan—under the leadership and authority of fathers. In this patriarchal society, political authority, personal property, and family line passed exclusively from father to son. In a very real sense, sons looked to their fathers for their identity and their livelihood, while fathers saw in their sons the means by which they extended themselves indefinitely into the future. All of this translated into a special bond between fathers and their sons, a relationship deeper than that commonly found in most modern cultures.

When the author spoke of God as a Father treating the Hebrew Christians as sons, his readers understood. They knew he meant that God behaved toward them as a benevolent authority figure who had a deep commitment to His people that He expressed in sovereignty and in love. Both of these concepts, sovereignty and love, constitute the dynamics behind the discipline of God. He rebukes them because He rules them. As a father, He has the authority and responsibility to punish His sons. At the same time, He disciplines them because He is devoted to them. As a father, He loves them and wants what is best for them. As between fathers and sons, so also between God and His people, this can necessitate the correction of an errant behavior or attitude.

The Father's Correction of His Children

Endure hardship as discipline . . . (Hebrews 12:7).

God disciplines us for our good, that we may share in his holiness. No discipline seems pleasant at the time, but painful. Later on, however, it produces a harvest of righteousness and peace for those who have been trained by it (Hebrews 12:10, 11).

The suffering of the righteous has always posed a serious challenge to vital faith in God. The idea of a just and loving God's presiding over human misery has never set well with those who are skeptical of religion. Believers, too, have taken exception to this great "injustice." As Oscar Wilde once observed, "There is enough misery on every street to disprove the existence of God."

Elie Wiesel, one of the many victims of the holocaust, remembers its horrors in his haunting book *Night*. A witness to man's greatest inhumanity to man, he sadly documents what it did to his faith in God. He arrived by train at Birkenbau to be greeted by the smell of burning humans:

> Never shall I forget that night, seven times cursed and seven times sealed. Never shall I forget that smoke. Never shall I forget the little faces of the children, whose bodies I saw turned into wreaths of smoke beneath a silent blue sky. Never shall I forget the nocturnal silence which deprived me, for all eternity, of the desire to live. Never shall I forget those moments which murdered my God and my soul and turned my dreams into dust. Never shall I forget these things, even if I am condemned to live as long as God Himself. Never.[23]

Just where is God in such suffering? Why does He permit it? Why does He allow bad things to happen to good people? The age-old question of Job now seems to be the question of the Hebrews. As the author moves in on this vital issue, he makes one of the most important contributions to the question of theodicy (justifying God's actions in His world) to be found in Scripture.

The Bible is not silent on this troubling subject. It speaks at length on the origin and role of suffering in God's world. In the opening

---

[23]Elie Wiesel, *Night* (New York: Avon Books, 1969), p. 9.

chapters of the book of Genesis, for example, suffering is portrayed as a malevolent intruder into a once benevolent world. It was not endemic to the world God created but entered that world as a consequence of human rebellion against God. According to Genesis 3, the anxiety, alienation, and physical hardship that characterize our human existence owe their origin, not to the creative act of God, but to the sin of humankind. Suffering is portrayed as both a natural consequence of sin and as the direct punishment of God upon sin. According to the Bible, fallen man lives in a world that is under a curse that manifests itself in suffering and death (Genesis 3:14ff; Romans 8:18-25).

The suffering-as-punishment model introduced in Genesis is also prominent in God's covenant relationship with Israel. Through Moses, God threatened Israel with all kinds of physical hardship should they fail to keep His commandments (e.g., Leviticus 26:14-39). Throughout Israel's history, the plague, the famine, and the hostile foe were "visited" upon them for their iniquities (e.g., Numbers 25; Judges 2:10ff). The prophets consistently explain the Babylonian invasion of Judah, with all of its death and destruction, as God's punishment of Judah's sin (e.g., Micah 3:9-12; Daniel 9:4-14; Ezekiel 33:27-29; Jeremiah 32:26-35).

So dominant is this suffering-as-punishment model in Scripture that some people think it to be the only Biblical explanation for the existence of human suffering. Nothing could be further from the truth. A closer examination of the Biblical statements on the subject reveals a number of alternative explanations to the phenomenon of suffering, some of which have nothing to do with human misbehavior. Job, for example, suffered not because of his sin, but, in a sense, because of his righteousness. According to the prologue of the book of Job, God permitted Satan to test the genuiness of Job's piety by depriving him, through suffering, of every tangible proof of God's providence—systematically taking away from him every self-serving reason to serve God. Job's unfair and unexplained suffering forces him to face God without reward or rationale, to do the good for goodness' sake, to serve God solely for who He is, rather than for what benefit it might bring to Job's life (cf. Job 2:8-12; 3:3-10). This is "suffering as trial," as test of faith and piety. It is the model of suffering James refers to when he says, "Consider it pure joy, my brothers, whenever you face trials of many kinds, because you know that the testing of your faith develops perseverance" (James 1:2, 3). It is what Peter means when he refers to the "painful trial" that his readers are suffering (1 Peter 4:12ff). It is what the Old Testament calls being "refined" or "tried" by the "fire" of hardship (Zechariah 13:9; Jeremiah 9:7).

Somewhat related to the suffering-as-trial model is the concept as suffering as a means to spiritual maturity. As noted above, James sees the Christian's struggle with suffering as a means to "perseverance" and "maturity" (James 1:2-4). This, too, is the claim of Paul: "We also rejoice in our sufferings, because we know that suffering produces perseverance; perseverance, character; and character, hope" (Romans 5:3, 4). As the Christian endures suffering, he learns to lean more upon God and thus grows in character, faith, and hope.

There is at least one additional Biblical model for explaining the meaning of human suffering. It is offered by Jesus as He prepares to perform one of His miracles. The disciples and Jesus encounter a man blind from birth. "Rabbi," His disciples ask, "who sinned, this man or his parents, that he was born blind?"

"Neither this man nor his parents sinned," replies Jesus, "but this happened so that the work of God might be displayed in his life." He then proceeds to heal the man (John 9:1ff).

According to Jesus, then, this man's suffering had nothing to do with sin, either his own or that of his parents. Instead, it served to provide an opportunity for Christ to display the works of God. We observe then, from this brief survey, that the Bible has more than one answer to question, "Why do people suffer?"

As we look for where the author's explanation of the suffering of the Hebrew Christians fits into this discussion, it is important that we note the following. First of all, this is not a discussion of the problem of pain in general. The author is not attempting a formal treatise on the origin of human misery and where God is in it. What he says on the subject is in specific response to the suffering of the Hebrews. Second, the suffering of the Hebrews is a direct result of their devotion to Christ. It is not the universal suffering of humankind that burdens them, but suffering in the form of religious persecution. This is what the author means by the phrase, "In your struggle against sin, you have not yet resisted to the point of shedding your blood" (Hebrews 12:4). What they are experiencing is akin to what Christ and a whole "host of witnesses" have endured, only to a lesser degree. The "hardship" in their lives is a direct result of their efforts to live for Christ in a hostile world.

The real issue here is the problem that their suffering poses for their faith. Here they are, attempting to do the Lord's will, and all they have to show for it is grief. They have suffered insult, confiscation of their property, and even imprisonment (Hebrews 10:32-34). They are fighting against an "enemy" who simply will not go away, and they are beginning to lose heart. Doubt is beginning to compromise their commitment—doubts about God's justice and His providence. What the author is trying to do is to reassure them that the suffering in their lives is not the result of God's rejection of them or His abandonment of them, but represents His efforts to discipline the children that He loves. This is suffering as a negative means to a positive end. God is permitting and even employing the persecution they are suffering to correct them and summon forth from them "holiness," "righteousness," and "peace" (Hebrews 12:10, 11).

C. S. Lewis once wrote, "God whispers to us in our pleasures; speaks in our consciences; but shouts in our pain." With that shout still ringing in their ears, the Hebrews are now learning one of the hardest lessons of the Christian life. The same God who is merciful and kind; who is patient and slow to anger; who is the giver of every good and perfect gift; is a God who "chastens" His children. "The Lord disciplines those he loves." Some people stumble over that theology. Not everybody can love a God who brings trouble; who allows bad things to happen to good people. "No discipline seems pleasant at the time." Because of this, some of God's children simply will not accept it. They brood, they smolder, they snarl, they seethe. Aiming a stubborn fist toward the sky, they go through life broken by bad breaks, forever demanding of God "Why?" and never having the faith to hear His answer.

The author of Hebrews has heard it, and he verily shouts it to the saints, "Later on, however, it produces a harvest of righteousness and peace." Rather than resent their suffering, he invites the Hebrews to reap from it—to come out of the heart of their trouble with a prize more fresh and fair than the unhurt, untroubled life can ever know.

Perhaps we should stay with Christ a while longer. Be assured of this—if you have not already learned it—God still disciplines those whom He loves. He will prick the plodding conscience and purge the prideful heart. He will soften the stubborn spirit and toughen the timid faith. He will deny and He will deprive. He will restrict and He will redirect. He will purify and He will probe. He will humble and He will hone. He will search and He will sharpen. He will test and He will try. He will wean us from this world. But, later on, it will bear the fruit of righteousness. What is sown in tears today will tomorrow be reaped in joy, and out of His chastening we will harvest character and peace.

"Soul-making" is what C. S. Lewis called it; the shaping of a Christian with the hammer and chisel of suffering. In the final analysis, why one suffers is not nearly as important as how one suffers. When approached from the perspective of faith, even the mystery and misery of pain can become a means to spirituality and a bridge to God.

Aleksandr Solzhenitsyn, himself a survivor of the concentration camps, testifies to how his suffering spurred him on to a new spirituality. One day, as he lay in a prison cell wrestling with the unfairness of it all, he learned a truth about himself that his "happier" days had been unable to teach him:

> It was only when I lay there on rotting prison straw that I sensed within myself the first stirrings of good. Gradually, it was disclosed to me that the line separating good and evil passes, not through states, nor between classes, nor between political parties either, but right through every human heart, and through all human hearts. So, bless you, prison, for having been in my life.[24]

Only a fool would pretend to understand suffering, and only a sadist would claim to enjoy it. But this at least can be said. There is in the struggles of life a catalyst for spiritual development that no other force can supply. Pain has the power to summon forth from us that which we find most difficult to surrender—uncompromising faith in God and unqualified love for God. It just so happens that in these very things, all true piety lies.

> In the still air the music lies unheard;
> In the rough marble beauty hides unseen.
> To make the music and the beauty, needs
> The master's touch, the sculptor's chisel keen.
> Great Master, touch us with thy skillful hand;
> Let not the music that is in us die!
> Great Sculptor, hew and polish us; let not,
> Hidden and lost, thy form within us lie!

---

[24]Aleksandr Solzhenitsyn, *The Gulag Archipelago* (New York: Harper & Row, 1975), Vol. II, p. 616.

Spare not the stroke! Do with us as thou wilt!
Let there be naught unfinished, broken, marred;
Complete thy purpose, that we may become
Thy perfect image, thou our God and Lord.[25]

[25]Horatius Bonar, as quoted in Maxie D. Dunnam, *Direction and Destiny* (New York: Abingdon Press, 1967), p. 25.

CHAPTER SIXTEEN

Living Outside the Camp

Hebrews 12:14—13:25

When Christopher Columbus returned from his historic voyage, he was asked to produce proof that he had indeed discovered a new route to the riches of the Orient. Among the many "treasures" he offered in evidence were some of the natives of the islands where he had landed, people whom he mistakenly called "Indians," after the country he thought he had found. Ironically, it was these very people who were to supply the first real evidence of a discovery even greater than the one Columbus thought he had made. This new kind of people became the crowning proof of his discovery of a whole new world.

In a sense, the same thing can be said of Christianity. The crowning proof of a genuine relationship with Jesus Christ is the emergence of a new kind of person—someone whose very life is lived as a testimony to their discovery of the Son of God. It is the proof that Christ himself chose: "By this all men will know that you are My disciples, if you have love for one another" (John 13:35, New American Standard Bible). The clear implication of that statement is that the life-style of the believers will be the identifying mark of their relationship to Jesus Christ. Fundamental to the New Testament portrait of Christianity is the expectation that those who believe in Christ will live a life that is distinctively "Christian" and thereby honor the One who has saved them.

Such is the premise behind this final section of the book of Hebrews. Like several other New Testament epistles, the book concludes by moving from the credenda to the agenda, from theological treatise to blueprint for Christian living. Finishing with a flurry of admonitions, the author begins to suggest the form that faith should take in the daily lives of the Hebrew Christians.

For the Hebrews, to live by faith in Jesus Christ as Son of God and great high priest meant that they must now go "outside the camp," beyond the confines of their traditional religion into a bold new arena of spiritual existence. For them, this was no small step. It had serious implications for almost every area of their lives. Family relationships, social acceptance, economic security, even personal freedom—all were put in jeopardy by the decision to follow the way of the cross. In a very real sense, the answer of Christ's call to salvation and service would require a whole new way of life. The author's characterization of that life in this the concluding section of the book represents for them, as it does for us, one of the New Testament's most compelling portraits of the faithful Christian life.

A Life Lived Unto God

> Since we are receiving a kingdom that cannot be shaken, let us be thankful, and so worship God acceptably with reverence and awe (Hebrews 12:28).

All dynamic Christian living begins with reverence for God. The fundamental theological principle of Scripture is that there is one true God who made all things and to whom all are accountable. Belief in such a God is presented as the foundation for human morality, the basis for all positive ethical behavior. According to the Bible, there can be no true piety apart from the reverence for a sovereign God.

Reverence for God has never come easy for rebellious humanity. Most people are too busy taking bows to bow before their Creator. Like our ancestors in the garden, irreverent humans still seem driven to "become gods" at God's expense. From the dawn of time, men have been posing as "gods" and bowing before the altars of their own invention. At the heart of all idolatry is an egotistical desire to worship some god made in the image of man. Even the church is not exempt of people who secretly bow before the god of self.

Such religion can never be truly Christian. Those who follow the "author and perfecter of our faith" follow One whose entire life was lived selflessly, in total submission to the will of the Father. His reverence for the Father translated into uncompromising commitment to God's agenda for His life (cf. Hebrews 5:7, 8; Philippians 2:5ff). Those who follow Him should be willing to do the same. To be a God-fearer, after the model of Christ, is to live all of life as if what God wishes is of ultimate consequence.

According to our author, such reverence for God expresses itself in three important ways. First, it manifests itself in obedience to

God's commands. That is his point in comparing the way Israel under Moses came to Mount Sinai with the way the church under Christ comes to Mount Zion, "the heavenly Jerusalem" (Hebrews 12:18-27). In the final warning of the book, he says, "If they did not escape when they refused him who warned them on earth, how much less will we, if we turn away from him who warns us from heaven?" (Hebrews 12:25). This is reverence as respect for God's authority, as fear of the consequences of our disobedience to His commands. The particular warning that the author has in mind is the same one he has sounded all along (e.g., Hebrews 3:12; 6:4-6; 10:26-39). It is what he here refers to as taking care not to miss the grace of God (Hebrews 12:15), that is, not to abandon faith in Christ and return to the ceremonialism and legalism of their former religion (cf. Hebrews 13:9-14).

A second way that reverence manifests itself is through holiness. At the heart of the Biblical idea of holiness is the concept of being set apart for, or belonging to, God. Biblically speaking, it has both ceremonial and moral implications. Here, the latter is implied, as it is when Peter writes, "But just as he who called you is holy, so be holy in all you do; for it is written: 'Be holy, because I am holy'" (1 Peter 1:15, 16; cf. Leviticus 19:2). In other words, when Christians live holy lives, they are bearing witness to God's ownership of their lives. They are identifying with their Lord and reflecting the moral excellence that is characteristic of God himself. Such a life, insists our author, is one of the prerequisites for the believer's approach to God (Hebrews 12:14b).

Now to some people, being set apart to God means literally to be set apart from the world. Not a few Christians have sought holiness behind the thick walls of religious asceticism or within the philosophical havens of theological mysticism. In fifth-century Antioch, there lived a man named Simeon Stylites, whose life serves as an example of the extremes to which some Christians have gone in their quest for personal holiness. Convinced that he could not be holy and still live in the world, Simeon sought to lift himself above the world. Tradition holds that he built a tower some sixty feet above the city, where he lived the last thirty years of his life in prayer and fasting.

Is that what it means to be holy? Not according to the author of Hebrews. His call for holiness comes not in the form of a challenge to live apart from the world, but in a challenge to live in the world with uncompromising faith and integrity. Trusting in God instead of material things and keeping oneself sexually pure are two specific examples he gives of what it means for the Christian to be in the world but not of the world. Such attitudes and actions constitute a form of holiness by which the believer identifies with his Lord and prepares himself to come into His presence (Hebrews 13:4-6).

A third manifestation of reverence in the Christian life mentioned in the text is the adoration of God in worship. According to the author of Hebrews, worship is something that we do both with our lips and with our lives. It expresses itself in "a sacrifice of praise—the fruit of lips that confess his name" (Hebrews 13:15). It also expresses itself in the desire "to do good and to share with others" (Hebrews 13:16). Thus, Christian worship is at its finest when it honors God and blesses men. Reverence for God calls Christians not just into the sanctuary, but beyond it. Like the character Faithful in *Pilgrim's Progress,* our faith enables us to sing not only in the Celestial City, but also in the Valley of the Shadow; and some poor soul stumbling on behind us thanks God and takes courage from our song to continue on his own pilgrimage of faith. Like Mother Theresa's, our reverence for God leads us outside the walls of the cathedral into the midst of the suffering masses to worship the Creator by ministering to the needs of His creatures. Even so, the author of Hebrews calls his readers to a life of love as the ultimate act of praise. "Real worship," says William Barclay,

> is the offering of everyday life to God. Real worship is not something that is transacted only in a church, real worship is something that sees the whole world as the temple of the living God; and every common deed as an act of worship.[26]

"With such sacrifices," says the author of Hebrews, "God is pleased" (Hebrews 13:16).

A Life Lived Unto Man

> Make every effort to live in peace with all men. . . . Keep on loving each other. . . . Do not forget to entertain strangers. . . . Remember those in prison. . . . Marriage should be honored by all. . . . Remember your leaders. . . . Share with others. . . . Pray for us (Hebrews 12:14; 13:1-4, 7, 16, 18).

26William Barclay, *The Letter to the Romans* (Philadelphia: Westminster Press), p. 169.

In the middle of the second century, the Athenian philosopher Aristides wrote to the Emperor Antonius Pius a description of the life-style of the earlier believers. The following is an excerpt:

> They walk in all humility and kindness and falsehood is not found among them. They love one another. They do not refuse to help widows. They rescue the orphans from violence. He who gives, gives ungrudgingly to him who lacks. When one of their poor passes from this world, any one of them who sees it provides for his burial. And if they hear that one of their members is in prison or oppressed for the name of their Messiah, all of them provide for his needs. Thus they labor to become righteous, as those who expect from him the glorious fulfillment of the promises made to them.[27]

This portrait of the life-style of the early believers bears a striking resemblance to one called for by the writer of Hebrews. In this final section of the book, the author addresses the one remaining question of his readers: "How should a faithful Christian live?" The answer he gives is the same one Jesus had given some years before: "Love one another." According to the author of Hebrews, the faithful Christian life is a life of love for humankind. Such a life, he insists, holds people in high esteem, listens attentively to their cries for help, and unselfishly ministers to their needs in the name of Jesus Christ.

Unfortunately, this is not the answer that some Christians want to hear. His call to a life of sacrificial ministry to the needs of people is certainly not in step with the prevailing mood of the me generation. Influenced by the selfishness of the materialistic age, many Christians today are more inclined to run from people's needs than they are to respond to them. Some believers face the needs of their fellow humans like the principal character in Shalom Aleichem's story of the man who did not want to get involved. It seems that an elderly man was standing on a crowded bus when a young man standing next to him asked, "What time is it?" The old man just turned away and refused to reply. After the young man moved on, the old man's friend asked him why he refused such a simple request. The old man answered, "If I had given him the time of day, next he would want to know where I was going. Then we might talk about our interests. If we did that, he might invite himself to my

---

[27]Aristedes, *Apology,* 15, 16.

house for dinner. If he did, he would meet my lovely daughter. If he met her, they would both fall in love. I don't want my daughter marrying someone who can't afford a watch."[28]

As absurd as that kind of reasoning is, it is just the kind of selfish logic that some Christians employ as an effective way to rationalize themselves out of any sense of social responsibility. With a kind of social paranoia, we greet every request of needful humanity with a cold calculation of what it might cost us and turn a deaf ear to the cry for help out of fear for the potential of overinvolvement. Or, even worse, we substitute pious language for meaningful ministry and so excuse ourselves of any further responsibility to the desperate needs of a suffering world. The problem that plagued the religion of ancient Israel still plagues the church. It is the tendency to associate piety with liturgy instead of life, to emphasize formal worship at the expense of genuine ministry to the needs of people. The result is a kind of "survivalist" mentality whereby the focus of the church has shifted from service to self-preservation, from meaningful ministry to maintenance of religious tradition.

This is not what the author has in mind in his call to faithful Christianity. His call to go "outside the camp" is not a call to self-preservation; it is a call to self-extinction. It is a call for the church to give itself away sacrificially unto the redemption of humanity. Pointing to Jesus, who "suffered outside the city gate to make the people holy through his own blood" (Hebrews 13:12), he calls the Hebrews to give of themselves in the same way, to humbly and unselfishly expend themselves unto the salvation and sanctification of their world.

What we have here is a new model of faithfulness to Jesus Christ—not measured in terms of church attendance and the practice of traditional piety, but measured in terms of sacrificial service to the people for whom Christ died. As George MacLeod, in his book *Only One Way Left,* says:

> What I am pleading for is that the cross of Christ be raised, not only on top of the church steeple, but also at the center of the market place. For Christ was not crucified between two candles on an altar, but between two thieves upon a cross. He was crucified upon the town garbage heap, where men talked smut and soldiers gambled. That's where he

---

28*Dynamic Preaching,* July, 1986, p. 7.

died, and that's what he died about—and that where the Church must be and what the Church must be about.[29]

It is an idea whose time has come. What the world needs from the church is not more liturgy but more love, not more church services but more Christian service. It needs people who will "go outside the camp," who will abandon the respectability and security of their traditional religion for the ignominious and precarious way of the cross. It needs people who by faith will intentionally and redemptively "lose their lives" in the service of their fellowmen.

In the summer of 1987, *Leadership* magazine had an article about an old missionary couple who were returning to the States to retire after many years of service in Africa. Their struggle with the meaning of their lives captures the very essence of the struggle of the Hebrew Christians. They had little money and no pension, and their health was broken. They were discouraged and afraid.

They soon discovered that they were booked on the same ship as President Teddy Roosevelt, who was returning from one of his big-game hunting expeditions.

> No one paid any attention to them. They watched the fanfare that accompanied the President's entourage, with passengers trying to catch a glimpse of the great man.
>
> As the ship moved across the ocean, the old missionary said to his wife, "Something is wrong. Why should we have given our lives in faithful service for God in Africa all these many years and have no one care a thing about us? Here this man comes back from a hunting trip and everybody makes much over him, but nobody gives two hoots about us."
>
> "Dear, you shouldn't feel that way," his wife said.
>
> "I can't help it; it doesn't seem right."
>
> When the ship docked in New York, a band was waiting to greet the President. The mayor and other dignitaries were there. The papers were full of the President's arrival, but no one noticed this missionary couple. They slipped off the ship and found a cheap flat on the East Side, hoping the next day to see what they could do to make a living in the city.

---

[29]George MacLeod, *Only One Way Left* (Glasgow: Iona Community, 1956), p. 148.

That night the man's spirit broke. He said to his wife, "I can't take this; God is not treating us fairly."

His wife replied, "Why don't you go in the bedroom and tell that to the Lord?"

A short time later he came out from the bedroom, but now his face was completely different. His wife asked, "Dear, what happened?"

"The Lord settled it with me," he said. "I told him how bitter I was that the President should receive this tremendous homecoming, when no one met us as we returned home. And when I finished, it seemed as though the Lord put his hand on my shoulder and simply said, 'But you're not home yet!'"[30]

And neither are we.

[30]*Leadership,* Summer, 1987, p. 48 (story condensed from Ray Stedman, *Talking to My Father*).

APPENDIX

Suggestions for Further Reading

It is our hope that this introduction to the Epistle to the Hebrews will stimulate the reader to undertake a deeper study of this important New Testament book. Listed below are some of the commentaries and special studies that might be useful in further research.

Adams, J. Clifford. "Exegesis of Hebrews VI. 1f." *New Testament Studies,* 13 (March, 1967), pp. 378-385.

Barclay, William. *The Letter to the Hebrews.* Philadelphia: Westminster Press, 1955.

Bruce, A. B. *The Epistle to the Hebrews.* Reprint. Minneapolis: Klock & Klock, 1980.

Bruce, F. F. *The Epistle to the Hebrews.* Grand Rapids: Eerdmans, 1964.

_____. "Recent Contributions to the Understanding of Hebrews." *The Expository Times,* 80 (September, 1969), pp. 260-264.

_____. "The Kerygma of Hebrews." *Interpretation,* 23 (January, 1969), pp. 3-19.

Buchanan, George Wesley. *To the Hebrews.* Garden City: Doubleday (Anchor Bible series), 1976.

Dods, Marcus. *The Epistle to the Hebrews.* Grand Rapids: Eerdmans (Expositor's Greek Testament series), 1964.

Evans, Louis H. *Hebrews.* Waco: Word (The Communicator's Commentary), 1985.

Guthrie, Donald. *The Letter to the Hebrews.* Grand Rapids: Eerdmans (Tyndale New Testament Commentaries), 1983.

Harrison, Everett F. "The Theology of the Epistle to the Hebrews," *Bibliotheca Sacra,* 121 (1964), pp. 333-340.

Howard, George. "Hebrews and the Old Testament Quotations," *Novum Testamentum,* 10 (February-March, 1968), pp. 208-216.

Kistemaker, Simon. *The Psalm Citations in the Epistle to the Hebrews.* Amsterdam: Wed. G. Van Soest N.V., 1961.

Lane, William L. *Hebrews: A Call to Commitment.* Peabody: Hendrickson Publishers, 1985.

Lenski, R. C. H. *The Interpretation of the Epistle to the Hebrews.* Columbus: Wartburg Press, 1946.

Lightfoot, Neil R. *Jesus Christ Today.* Grand Rapids: Baker Book House, 1976.

Milligan, Robert. *A Commentary on the Epistle to the Hebrews.* Reprint. Nashville: Gospel Advocate, 1975.

Nairne, Alexander. *The Epistle to the Hebrews.* Cambridge: University Press, 1921.

Robinson, Theodore H. *The Epistle to the Hebrews.* New York: Harper and Brothers (Moffatt New Testament Commentaries), n.d.

Stewart, R. A. "The Sinless High-Priest," *New Testament Studies,* 14 (January, 1967), pp. 126-135.

Stott, Wilflrid. "The Conception of 'Offering' in the Epistle to the Hebrews," *New Testament Studies,* 9 (January, 1962), pp. 62-67.

Swetnam, James. "A Suggested Interpretation of Hebrews 9:15-18," *Catholic Biblical Quarterly,* 27 (April, 1965), pp. 373-390.

Thompson, James. *The Letter to the Hebrews.* Austin: Sweet, 1971.

Vos, Geerhardus. *The Teaching of the Epistle to the Hebrews.* Grand Rapids: Eerdmans, 1956.

Wilson, R. McLean. *Hebrews.* Grand Rapids: Eerdmans (New Century Bible Commentaries), 1987.